Lead Like a Legend

The 5 C's That Unlock Greatness

By

Ryan Stream

Table of Contents

Introduction 1

Chapter 1: Choice 5

Chapter 2: Clarity 17

Chapter 3: Consistency 29

Chapter 4: Connection 39

Chapter 5: Courage 55

Chapter 6: 10 Days 72

Chapter 7: How to Beat the Ten-Day Fade 76

Chapter 8: What Real Leaders Do Differently 80

Chapter 9: Be the One 83

Chapter 10: Rise, Champion 88

Chapter 11: Letter to Self 95

Bonus Chapter: Fuel for the Fight — Quotes to Lead, Rise, and Dominate 99

Introduction

This isn't just a book. It's a map of the path I walked—from brokenness to battle-tested. From a kid who didn't know his real father, who bounced between homes, even slept in a homeless shelter, and pain, oh so much pain—to a man who learned how to build businesses, raise a family, speak on stages, accept music awards and write books, I learned from other leaders how to lead like a legend.

You won't find fluff here. What you will find are principles forged in real life. Tools, not theories. Truth, not hype.

I'm sharing with you the 5 C's I learned that led me to leading like a legend.:

- Choice
- Clarity
- Consistency
- Connections
- Courage

You'll find that these are more than ideas—they're actions. They sum up how I personally lead my family, my business, my team, and myself, and I hope they will help you lead like a legend too, in whatever you are pursuing.

You might be a CEO, a teacher, a soldier, a coach, a parent, or a student with big dreams. Whoever you are—this book is for you.

Introduction

Because the truth is: **Leaders aren't born. They're built.** And this book will help build the leader in you.

Yes—*you.*
The one reading this right now.
You can absolutely be a legendary leader.

Hear me out.
God didn't misplace you.
You weren't born in the wrong time.
You weren't called to be average.
You were forged for *this* exact moment in history.

You've survived battles that were meant to break you.
You've heard the lies: "You're not ready. You're not enough. You're too broken. You're not smart enough."
But here you are—still standing. Still breathing. Still burning.
Still fanning that spark inside you by picking up this book.

You're not here to blend in.
You're here to build, to break chains, to lead.

You are the answer to someone's prayer.
You're a warrior in a world full of watchers.
A leader in a time starving for truth.
Not because you're perfect—because you said yes.

This book is a call to arms.
A map for living with fire, leading with purpose, and building a legacy that echoes beyond your name.

Introduction

These stories are real. They're raw. And the Five C's I learned from them work.

In this book you'll learn all about what it really takes to rise. To lead with integrity. To build something that lasts.

But why read this particular book? Well, I was the idiot. The one labeled the dumb ass that couldn't read their name. The drug addict, the short boy, the misfit and safety liability. You name it, I've have been called it but now? Now I own businesses, have degrees and awards and can support all my family's needs. Does that make me a better person than you? No. It just means I had good leaders in my life, and I watched them.

Lead Like a Legend: The 5 C's That Unlock Greatness

Welcome to the 5 C's!
This is where leaders are made, and legends rise.

This book is not the story of my early years of homelessness. It's not about living in foster care... losing my mother to suicide... falling into addiction... going to jail... or going to war twice and nearly ending my own life.

If you want to read that story—my fight from rock bottom to redemption—check out my first book: Conquering Your Colosseum: A raw, real guide on self-evaluation, accountability, belief, making a plan, and taking action.

Or check out the story I share with my wife, Elizabeth, in: I Feel Like a Giant It's a powerful book on confidence—featuring nine steps to building it from the inside out. It also tells my wife's story: of coming to America and not knowing English, and our experiences together through heartbreak, healing, and ultimately, helping others grow.

But this book? This one is for the leaders. The builders. The people who want to make an impact—not just once, but every day. The students, entrepreneurs, soldiers, teachers, CEOs, and dreamers who are tired of the hype and are hungry for habits... truth... and results.

And yes—I may sprinkle in some stories from my past. Not for sympathy. Not for drama. But because my past taught me the power of the Five C's. I didn't learn these in a classroom—I learned them in combat, in prison, in recovery, and in business.

Chapter 1

Choice

"Everything starts with a choice."

Before we get into everything 'leadership', I've got a question for you:

Who are the greatest people of all time? Think about it. What names come to mind? Why were they great? What did they do—and what kind of leadership qualities made them unforgettable?

Let's break it down.

If we're talking about the last one hundred years, a quick Google search will hit you with names like:

- **Martin Luther King Jr.** — Led a movement for civil rights with nonviolence and unshakable conviction.
- **Henry Ford** — Revolutionized the auto industry by inventing the assembly line.
- **Steve Jobs** — Transformed technology by merging innovation with vision.
- **Elon Musk** — Took risks and reimagined space, energy, and transportation.

- **Michael Jordan** — Redefined greatness through a relentless work ethic and fierce competitiveness.

They're all involved in different arenas—civil rights, industry, tech, space, and sports. But they all had/have one thing in common: they made bold, intentional choices that shaped history.

Now let's go back even further:

- **Jesus Christ** — A spiritual leader who taught love, forgiveness, and servant leadership. Billions follow His teachings today.
- **The Prophet Muhammad** — A prophet and statesman who united the Arabian Peninsula through faith, discipline, and vision.
- **Albert Einstein** — A physicist who unlocked the mysteries of the universe and reshaped modern science with his theory of relativity.
- **Genghis Khan** — A fearless conqueror who built one of the largest empires in history through strategy, discipline, and ruthlessness.
- **Alexander the Great** — A military genius who led from the front, uniting much of the known world before the age of thirty.
- **The Buddha** — A spiritual teacher who rejected wealth and status to pursue enlightenment—his teachings still impact billions seeking peace and purpose.

They all had different beliefs. Different missions. Different methods. But again, every one of them made decisions that shifted generations.

Real Talk: The Legends Behind the Legends

Back in the day, society operated differently. Men and women often had clearly defined roles—not because one was more important than the other, but because that was the cultural norm. Men were pushed into the spotlight. Women were expected to hold it all together behind the scenes.

But just because a person wasn't in front of the camera or on the front page doesn't mean they weren't making history.

Fact:

Throughout every century, women have changed the world—as scientists, warriors, writers, queens, abolitionists, inventors, civil rights leaders, and more.

But history books haven't always been fair.

Too many didn't get the credit they deserved.

Too many names were lost, buried, or never written down at all.

Still, their fingerprints are everywhere.

Let's not forget the women who:
- Raised the leaders
- Sacrificed their bodies, time, and energy for the next generation

- Built homes, communities, and character when no one was clapping
- Fought battles of the heart, the home, and the world

They weren't just behind the scenes—they were building the stage.

They didn't just support greatness—they created it.

So yeah, history might not have given them the spotlight

But we will.

And, now that things have changed, women are doing amazing things and getting the credit they deserve!

Now... what is greatness, really?

Greatness is the relentless pursuit of excellence. It's driven by passion, integrity, and the fire to make the world better. Even when no one is there to witness it. When no one claps your performance. Even when it costs you something. And it always—always—starts with a choice.

Think about it. You've already made dozens of choices today. What to wear. What to eat. Whether to show up or stay stuck.

Let's be real. I'm not saying you need to lead armies across deserts, heal the blind, build rockets, or invent the next AI empire. That's been done. That's someone else's story. And now, this is yours. So... what will you build?

Lead Like a Legend: The 5 C's That Unlock Greatness

Your life is built by your choices. Not your circumstances. Not your past. Not what someone did to you—or what someone failed to give you.

It's the choices you make—and the ownership you take—that shape your future.

And it doesn't matter where you work or what your title is. Every job, every relationship, every day comes with choices.

For example, in mining, it's safety or shortcuts. Pride or passivity. Excellence or average.

In healthcare, it's compassion or coldness. Presence or burnout. Teamwork or ego.

In transportation, it's focus or distraction. Responsibility or blame. Discipline or drifting.

In construction, it's precision or laziness. Respect or conflict. Finish strong or give up.

In technology, it's solved problems or make excuses. Integrity or shortcuts. Adapt or fall behind.

In education, it's inspired or instruct. Lead or lecture. Connect or clock out.

And in life, i's always the battle between what's easy and what's right.

You don't need a title to lead. Leaders are the ones who make better choices, more consistently.

Choice

I made a choice as a kid that changed everything.

I remember seeing my mom's face bloodied. Hurt. And thinking, *who did this to her? Why?*

That day, I made a choice: I was going to be someone strong. Someone others could count on. Someone people could run to if they needed help.

But not all of my choices were good ones.

I chose the wrong roads: drinking. Drugs. Skipping school. Life after war. Lying to my wife. I made choices that led to consequences I never wanted.

That's the thing about choice. You get to pick the action... but you don't get to pick the consequence.

You choose the shortcut? You get the setback. Not being safe at work or having your mind off task.? If you choose dishonesty, you get distrust. If you choose distraction, you lose direction.

Eventually, I was labeled: A liability. Unsafe. Unaccountable. A man headed toward brokenness, divorce, and regret.

In this country, 49 percent of marriages end in divorce. We're the most advanced nation on earth... yet we're breaking down in our homes!

So, what needs to change?

Here's what I believe: People need to realize they're already leaders.

Yes—you. You lead yourself through this life. Your mom and dad might help for the first eighteen years (if you're lucky) … But after that? It's on you. And the sooner we take responsibility for our lives, the sooner you can step and be the leader you already are inside.

In my first book, I talked about five things that changed everything:

- Self-evaluation
- Accountability
- Self-belief
- Making a plan
- Taking action

But all of those things start with a choice.

The moment I said, "I'm done with not achieving. I'm going to be great. It's not over until I win! "That's when my life began to change. It started with a choice to believe it was possible.

I didn't start this new life of mine guessing what to do. I started listening to the Eric Thomases, Les Browns of the world, Tim Grover—and I didn't know at the time that years later, I'd be in the same room and on some of the same stages with them! Anything is possible, my friends.

When I started reading about the legends, the giants., I realized something key:

Learning Point: To become a legend… You've got to *learn from the legends.*

Choice

Whether you like them or not—your opinion doesn't cancel their impact. They were great because they chose to be.

And if you want to lead like a legend... as I said already, it all starts with a choice.

Some people choose a poor mindset. They pass over opportunities again and again—and then get mad that life isn't going their way.

I'll tell you straight up. This isn't a book about meditation or working out. Or getting up at 5 am. Although all those things are great.

Let's be real right now—the way you look, feel, and move is a direct reflection of your choices and daily habits.

I want you to think about your spirit. Where's it at? What about your energy? Your vibe? Your glow? Your aura? Would you want to be around you?

It all comes back to one thing: CHOICE.

I'll be clear—after you make the choice, it doesn't mean your life magically shifts like blowing out birthday candles and poof—your dreams come true.

Once you choose to change, you get change. And yep—change is hard. The best rewards never come easy!

I mean, I went from losing my job, crying at the VA Medical Center, looking for the enemy in my own home. My wife sat on the edge of our bed in tears, saying, "Ryan, the enemy is not in our backyard."

I'll be completely honest with you. There were the nights I was punching holes in the walls like a child… because I *chose* not to get help. My help didn't come in some shiny moment, either. Nope, it's not like in the story books. My help came through *choosing* to go to family counseling. And it came through listening to the voices of people the world labeled as great. The leaders I was listening to, their words reminding me I still had worth and that my choices still mattered.

That's what this is about. *Choosing* healing. *Choosing* growth. Choosing to lead yourself before you lead anyone else.

My dear friends—I think I've drummed it in enough now: it starts with choice. But what will you choose?

What job? How will you act? How will you treat people? Do you want the nice body or the bag of Cheetos?

The truth is—a lot of people don't even know what they want. They stop dreaming, almost like they think the world will just bless them with a perfect family, nice car, steady income, and a happily-ever-after. Sadly, it doesn't' happen that way and many of us wake up one and wonder why our dream hasn't come true.

I remember graduating high school, tossing my hat in the air, and thinking life was just going to hand me success. Why? Because I was a nice guy. I had a lot of friends. A good smile. I was funny!

If only life worked that way, right?

The point is this: If you don't know what you want, you'll end up with whatever life gives you. Not what you dreamed of—just what you can get.

Unfortunately, a lot of people are depressed. It's easy to see why. They're spending their lives chasing someone else's dreams. Clocking in for someone else's vision. Living on autopilot in jobs they hate, paying for someone else's dream life.

And all because they didn't choose to go after what they really wanted. They settled. They took what they could get, hoping for the dream that never came.

But *you* don't have to.

You can choose the job. You can choose to be safe. You can choose to listen to those who made it and learn from them. You can choose to lead. You can choose to make a difference—for yourself, your team, and your family.

Choosing all those wonderful things won't guarantee constant happiness. That's not real life. There's no such thing, for anyone. But you know what *is* real? Progress.

Learning Point: The opposite of depression isn't happiness—it's *progression*.

When you choose to work toward something—*anything* that matters to you, life becomes rewarding.

Before we dive into Clarity, number two in our 5 C's, let me leave you with one more powerful story about choice.

Lead Like a Legend: The 5 C's That Unlock Greatness

There's a coach from BYU named Kalani Sitake. On a podcast, he shared something about his father that really stuck with me.

He said: "I'll tell you a quick story about my father—the man who raised me. He struggled. We had a lot of jobs. Then one night, he told me, 'I need your help.'

We walked into a trashed office building—papers everywhere, broken furniture, anger still in the air. People were upset about the layoffs. My dad said, 'New ownership. Layoffs. Our job is to clean it up.'

As we cleaned, he told me stories about every person who used to work there—what they meant to him. Hours later, after we finished cleaning the whole place, I said, 'Pops, I'm glad you still have the keys.'

He looked at me and said, 'Oh, I left them on the desk. Today was Daddy's last day.'

That man lost his job—but he chose to show up. He chose to clean that place like it was still his. He chose to let me be part of that moment. That's the man who raised me."

Coach Sitake ended by saying something that hit my soul: "Kindness is a superpower my dad had."

That right there is leadership. Ownership. Pride. Humility. Choice.

Imagine if more men and women showed up like that—in their lives, in their jobs, in their families. Imagine the ripple effect of

Choice

choosing integrity even when no one's watching. That kind of choice changes everything.

I want you to ask yourself—what would life look like if you showed up like that? Would your team be stronger? Would your kids feel safer? Would your story start shifting?

And now, with that story in your mind and heart—

Let's talk about what comes after the choice…

Clarity.

Chapter 2

Clarity

"If your crew isn't clear, mistakes happen."

My job is to teach how to cut through the noise, create clear goals on and off the jobsite, and communicate with precision so every person knows their role, their value, and their mission.

I don't care how strong you are, how motivated, or how much potential you have—if you don't have *clarity*, you're just busy being busy. You're running fast... in the wrong direction.

When I talk about clarity, I'm not referring to simply knowing what you want. I mean cutting through all the distractions, confusion, and noise—on the job, at home, and in your own head.

When I speak to teams, I say this: "If you don't know your role, you'll guess. And guessing leads to mistakes."

The same thing goes for life. If you don't know your purpose, your mission, your values... you'll guess them. You'll follow trends. Follow pressure. Follow people. Float along like everyone else and end up who knows where.

And guess what? You'll also end up frustrated, tired, and way off course.

Clarity

Leaders don't stumble into greatness. They build it with intention. And that starts with clarity.

So, what is clarity, exactly?

Clarity is like a perfectly clean window. When it's clean, you can see exactly what's on the other side. No streaks. No smudges. No confusion. Just direction.

If you want to accomplish a dream, if you want to hit a goal—you need clarity. You need to see exactly what you're aiming for. It sounds simple but it's amazing how many people are driving along the story of their lives with a blurry windscreen.

And you need to know every step it takes to get where you want to go.

In your work, clarity means knowing your role, your goal, and the standard you live by. In your relationships, clarity means being honest—about your expectations, your communication, and your intentions.

In your leadership, clarity means being real with your people—no guessing, no mixed messages, no "maybe."

Clarity makes the mission simple. Not easy—but simple. Because when you're clear, you stop reacting to life—and start leading it. Let me repeat that because it's so key at this point: when you're clear, you stop reacting to life and start leading it.

In 2017, I experienced some real clarity.

Lead Like a Legend: The 5 C's That Unlock Greatness

I was let go from my job, I almost lost my marriage, and I failed out of college. After failing out of college four times, (yes, four times), I got back in—on a mission. Not just to prove people wrong, but to prove to myself that if I followed the steps in this book—the same ones you're reading now—I could build a life worth admiring. Worth being proud of.

I got clear. I decided I wanted to be a motivational speaker, a musician, a best-selling author, and an entrepreneur.

Some people laughed. Rap music and country? Building businesses and getting a degree? I was the guy who once had a 1.3 GPA and got fired.

Fast forward seven years:

I worked a weekend shift in the mining industry. I put every bit of overtime into flipping real estate. I used a home equity line of credit to invest in property. I sold those homes and went in on an ice cream franchise. I retired from the military. I started a trucking company. My wife launched Stream Beauty. We built a nonprofit: A Smile in Every Classroom. I wrote two books and started a third: Heroes on the Playground. I earned a degree in psychology and family science. I've spoken in thirty-two states, combining rap, country, storytelling, and leadership. And now, besides writing this, I'm working towards a higher degree.

Learning Point: There is no cheat code to success. There is clarity.

Clarity

It starts by identifying exactly what you want to do—being specific—and then attacking those steps with everything you've got.

Jim Rohn said it best: "If you want to be a bread maker, go to the bread maker."

My friends, that's clarity. If you want to know something—go to the source. Get some clear steps from the people doing what you want to do.

Clarity isn't complicated. It's critical.

Let me give you another example. I didn't just learn the After-Action Review in the military—I lived it. In Afghanistan, there was no room for "maybes." No room for vagueness. We had to be clear, concise, and committed—before stepping outside the wire, and after coming back.

We got briefed on what was supposed to happen. And no matter how the mission turned out, we ran it back with brutal honesty:

ARMY AAR -

What was supposed to happen? (What was the mission, goal, or plan?)

What actually happened? (What really went down — the good, the bad, and the unexpected?)

What can we do better next time? (What are the lessons learned? What changes will we make moving forward?)

Lead Like a Legend: The 5 C's That Unlock Greatness

I was let go from my job, I almost lost my marriage, and I failed out of college. After failing out of college four times, (yes, four times), I got back in—on a mission. Not just to prove people wrong, but to prove to myself that if I followed the steps in this book—the same ones you're reading now—I could build a life worth admiring. Worth being proud of.

I got clear. I decided I wanted to be a motivational speaker, a musician, a best-selling author, and an entrepreneur.

Some people laughed. Rap music and country? Building businesses and getting a degree? I was the guy who once had a 1.3 GPA and got fired.

Fast forward seven years:

I worked a weekend shift in the mining industry. I put every bit of overtime into flipping real estate. I used a home equity line of credit to invest in property. I sold those homes and went in on an ice cream franchise. I retired from the military. I started a trucking company. My wife launched Stream Beauty. We built a nonprofit: A Smile in Every Classroom. I wrote two books and started a third: Heroes on the Playground. I earned a degree in psychology and family science. I've spoken in thirty-two states, combining rap, country, storytelling, and leadership. And now, besides writing this, I'm working towards a higher degree.

Learning Point: There is no cheat code to success. There is clarity.

Clarity

It starts by identifying exactly what you want to do—being specific—and then attacking those steps with everything you've got.

Jim Rohn said it best: "If you want to be a bread maker, go to the bread maker."

My friends, that's clarity. If you want to know something—go to the source. Get some clear steps from the people doing what you want to do.

Clarity isn't complicated. It's critical.

Let me give you another example. I didn't just learn the After-Action Review in the military—I lived it. In Afghanistan, there was no room for "maybes." No room for vagueness. We had to be clear, concise, and committed—before stepping outside the wire, and after coming back.

We got briefed on what was supposed to happen. And no matter how the mission turned out, we ran it back with brutal honesty:

ARMY AAR -

What was supposed to happen? (What was the mission, goal, or plan?)

What actually happened? (What really went down — the good, the bad, and the unexpected?)

What can we do better next time? (What are the lessons learned? What changes will we make moving forward?)

Lead Like a Legend: The 5 C's That Unlock Greatness

Sustain and improve: What worked? What didn't?

That process saved lives. But it also built leaders.

And here's the truth: I didn't leave that clarity in the combat zone. I brought it back—with me, on stage, into college classrooms, into boardrooms, and behind the wheel of a trucking company I started with zero experience.

When I a stepped on the stage for the first time as a speaker, I reviewed the experience like it was a mission.

When I went back to school after a tough childhood, deployments, and doubt? I applied that same clarity and courage I learned from those military briefings.

When I started a business and didn't know what a DOT number was? I didn't panic—I adapted. I learned fast. I checked my progress. I adjusted and I figured it out.

Now, for thirteen years, I was a military miner. And I spent those years dreaming about something more: Speaking. Rapping. Building something that mattered.

I bet you've had dreams too. You don't need all the answers to get started. You need the courage to take action, one step at a time. You need the clarity to know where you're going and the consistency to check in, adjust, and get better every step of the way.

Clarity

Now, let's circle back to some of the greatest people of all time. What did they all have in common? Clarity. A mission. A reason to keep going when everything around them told them to stop.

Take Genghis Khan, for example. The man who would one day conquer more land than any ruler in history. He started as a poor boy. With no crown. No castle. No chance.

His father was murdered. His tribe abandoned him. He literally had to hunt rats to survive.

But what made him different from anyone else in the same position as him? It wasn't money. It wasn't luck. It was vision, clarity, and relentless leadership.

First of all, he united the tribes that hated each other. He built systems. He built armies. He built an amazing legacy that still echoes today.

So, don't tell me you can't build something because you're broke, overlooked, abandoned, or undereducated.

If Genghis Khan can go from a starving boy to a world conqueror, you can go from a dreamer to a doer to a difference-maker. To a whatever-it-is you want.

I'm no warlord, but I am a warrior. I went from homeless to hopeful. From foster care to father. From battlefield to business owner. From a nobody with a notebook to a speaker on a mission.

So, the next time you doubt yourself, remember: Even Genghis Khan started as a poor boy with little prospects.

Learning Point: where you start doesn't define you—what you choose, and how clearly you see your mission, does. Choice. Clarity.

Now let's look at the other side of leadership—not through war, but through love.

The Greatest Name in History — What Jesus Taught Me About Clarity and Leadership

If you were to Google "Who is the most well-known name in human history?" One name rises above all others: Jesus Christ.

Love Him or not. Believe in Him or not. The numbers don't lie.

He's the most recognized figure on the planet! His name has endured and inspired through over 2,000 years of history. His words have shaped nations, cultures, calendars, and billions of lives.

And here's the wild part:

He never led an army. Never held political office. Never wrote a book. He walked. He talked. He served. He *loved*. And an army of hearts followed Him.

This isn't about religion. This isn't about what you believe. I've served in countries where people would strap bombs to their bodies because of what they believed.

This is deeper than belief — this is about choice, influence, clarity, and leadership that lasts. Here's a breakdown the leadership of Jesus:

1. **He Had Clarity of Identity:** He knew who He was. There was no confusion. No ego. No pretending. People follow leaders who are anchored in something bigger than themselves.
2. **He Spoke with Clarity:** He didn't confuse or complicate. He taught in parables — simple, clear stories that pierced the heart. "Love your neighbor." "Let your yes be yes and your no be no." He shows that the most powerful messages are often the simplest.
3. **He Led Through Service:** He washed people's feet. He fed the hungry. He spent time with the broken, the outcasts, the forgotten. People didn't follow Him because they were forced to. They followed Him because He showed up for them.
4. **He Inspired Through Sacrifice:** He didn't ask others to do what He wasn't willing to do Himself. He gave everything — including His life — for His mission. That's choice. That's leadership. That's clarity. That's courage.

What else can we learn from Him? Know who you are. Clarity starts with identity. If you're not clear, your team won't be clear either.

Keep it simple. Say what you mean. Mean what you say.

Serve first. Leadership isn't about power. It's about people.

Live the mission. Don't just preach the vision — bleed for it.

Jesus didn't need a crown to lead like a king. He didn't need an army to change the world. He made a choice to live the way he did, he had clarity, purpose, courage — and a message that couldn't be silenced.

And that's the kind of leadership this world needs more of.

Are you ready to lead like that?

Clarity at the Plate: The Story of the "Little Guy" Who Made It Big

They called him too small. Too short. Too slow. Too unlikely to ever make it.

But none of that mattered — because this kid had something that most people never find. You guessed it: clarity.

From a young age, he knew exactly what he wanted.

"I'm going to play in the MLB."

He didn't say maybe. He didn't say I'll try. He said it with fire, with conviction, with crystal-clear certainty.

But the world didn't believe in him.

He was the little guy — so short and scrawny, he didn't even look like an athlete. Coaches overlooked him. Scouts passed him by. But he wasn't chasing attention — he was chasing purpose.

So, what did he do?

He asked to be the bat boy. Yup. That was his choice. He just wanted to be near the game. High school? Bat boy. College? Bat boy again.

Clarity

He carried equipment before he carried a bat. He served water before he served fastballs over the fence.

Why? Because his mission was clear. And clarity gives you the patience to prepare while you wait for your moment.

And that moment came.

Fast forward. He finally got his shot. The Boston Red Sox called him up.

Game 1. His first-ever at-bat in the major leagues...

He hits a home run!

Boom. Just like that — the little guy who was too short, too slow, and too often doubted went yard. From bat boy to the big leagues. From overlooked to unstoppable.

His name? Dustin Pedroia.

AL Rookie of the Year MVP 2x World Series Champion

A walking map of clarity, grit, and heart.

So why am I sharing this particular story? Because you don't need to be big to be bold. You don't need permission to pursue your mission. And you don't have to be the first one picked — you just must be the one who never quits.

Dustin didn't wait for the spotlight. He showed up in the shadows — because he was clear on where he was going.

That's what clarity does. It keeps you grounded when you're overlooked… And it launches you when it's your turn to swing.

My First At-Bat

I remember the first time I was given sixty minutes on stage as a public speaker. I was fired up. But guess what?

I forgot my own music and I literally read my speech off a piece of paper. I felt silly… like a little guy who didn't belong up there.

But deep down — I just knew: One day… It's going to happen.

I started practicing and rehearsed my speeches and music in empty baseball fields and rodeo arenas — imagining the crowd, seeing the stage, hearing the applause.

Did I hit a home run after that? Nope. Not even close!

I paid a few thousand dollars to fly to Chicago and showcase for a bunch of colleges. And when they called my name for the first time ever on that type of stage — my computer happened to get itself unplugged and died as I was walking up.

I couldn't believe it. *Really, God?* I asked.

The organizers had to skip me, and the next guy got took to the stage instead.

I ran all over the hotel looking in my room and the lounge for my charger. It was right there by the computer, in the stand next to the tech guy.

It was finally my turn to take the stage… and I failed.

Clarity

Yep, my first corporate event was a failure.

Sure, I got a few handshakes and a few kind words. But guess what? It wasn't all bad.

I was just getting started. I needed the repetitions. The swings. And the misses.

I knew it wasn't about perfection. It was about clarity — knowing my mission and then leaning into the 3rd C — *Consistency* — to carry me through the grind.

So, no, I didn't hit a home run my first time on stage. But I kept showing up. I kept swinging. I kept improving.

When you're clear on where you're going... and consistent in how you show up... even the little guy can knock it out of the park.

Chapter 3

Consistency

> "Anyone can show up strong once. But I teach the mindset that builds consistency—the habit of showing up strong, focused, and reliable every single day. That's how you build trust, teams, and legacy."

Now, no one learns how to walk by watching YouTube tutorials.

We learn by falling.

And guess what? A baby falls an average of seventeen times an hour while learning to walk. Seventeen times, every hour. And they still get back up. Over and over. No excuses. No overthinking. Just grit in diapers.

Nobody tells that baby, "Maybe walking just isn't for you."

The same goes for talking. Riding a bike. Reading. Writing. Driving. Lifting. Leading.

We master these things through consistency. Through trying—and through not giving up.

You know what else? Some people learn faster than others. That's okay. Don't compare yourself to others. Comparison is the thief of joy. Beware of it. What matters isn't your pace—it's your persistence.

Consistency

But keep this in mind: we all have to work.

Success doesn't come from talent, and it doesn't come from luck.

It comes from reps, from rhythm, from resilience.

Somewhere along the way, as adults, we forget that. We let failure mess with our identity. We fall once and think it defines us. We miss a day and convince ourselves we're not disciplined. We start something good, and when it doesn't blow up instantly—we quit.

Let me tell you something right now:

Missing a day doesn't make you a failure. Quitting does.

Success isn't sexy.

It's not shiny. It's not viral.

It's invisible.

It's created in early mornings, quiet decisions, and small habits stacked over time.

Learning Point: *Consistency* is what builds everything that matters. It builds trust. It builds strength. It builds identity.

I've said it before, and I'll say it again: this has nothing to do with perfection. It's about presence. It's about showing up over and over again. It's about being someone your team, your family, your future can count on.

That means when life hits hard—you reset. When you fall short—you review. When you lose someone, when you lose momentum, when the fire dies out—you don't retreat. You return.

Life's going to punch you, okay. Hard. Nobody is exempt from pain, loss, fear, heartbreak, or struggle. That's just how it is.

But when we fall off the wagon—whether it's with our health, our habits, our marriage, our leadership, our finances, or our faith—we don't have to stay there. We get back up. We return to the mission.

And we do that with consistency.

You might think that being consistent is hard. But when you stop being consistent—your body gets tight. Your health declines. Your marriage drifts. Your bank account suffers. Your spiritual life gets dry. That's a whole lot harder. Choose your hard.

Consistency will keep you moving forward, and it'll also keep you from sliding backward. It's like oxygen to your goals. To your fire. You don't always notice it—but without it, everything fades.

Consistency builds leaders. Leaders build teams.

I think you can answer this for me now: When the wheels fall off—what do we do? We go back to what we learned in Chapter One: Choice.

We choose to change.

Then we return to Chapter Two: Clarity.

Consistency

We get crystal clear on what we want and why we want it.

Then we step into Chapter Three: Consistency.

We keep on going, because nothing grows without it.

From what I've observed, many people are consistent, but in the *wrong direction*. This is not necessarily bad. They're just misaligned. They consistently feed doubt. Consistently chase money. Consistently put their energy into titles and things that don't fuel their spirit. There's no clarity to their consistency, you see.

Remember, where your mind goes, your body follows.

That's why your thoughts, your habits, and your daily mindset matter. Manifestation isn't magic—it's momentum. You're always creating something with your actions. The question is, what are you consistently building?

At most events I speak at, people care deeply about business and money. I see it all the time. You meet someone and it's always:

"Hello." "What's your name?" "Where are you from?" "What do you do?"

And based on that third question—we categorize them. Psychology tells us we do this automatically. We place people above or below us in an instant.

We forget that there are far more important questions, such as:

- How's their mental health?

- How's their family?
- Do they sleep well at night?
- What would their children say about them?
- Are they healthy? Happy? Honest?

Many people are so focused on wealth, they neglect their wellness. I see it in the crowd. I see it on the stage. Even my own friends—millionaires—pay other people just to teach them how to stay fit. They're rich in money, but bankrupt in energy or in what matters most.

The Last March of Alexander the Great

Let me share a story.

Alexander the Great.

The name sounds like thunder—like a war drum pounding through history. The young Macedonian king who conquered the known world by thirty years of age. From Greece to Egypt to India. A military genius. A warrior. A living legend.

But at just thirty-two, Alexander fell ill in Babylon. Some say it was malaria. Some say it was poison. Either way—death came for him like it comes for us all. But oh, so early.

And as he lay on his deathbed, Alexander didn't ask for treasure. He didn't brag about his conquests. He gave his generals his three final wishes:

1. Let the best doctors carry my coffin.
2. Scatter all my wealth—my gold, silver, jewels—on the road to my grave.

Consistency

3. Leave my hands hanging outside the coffin.

His generals were stunned. "Why, my King?" they asked.

Alexander whispered:

"I want the world to know… even the best doctors cannot save you from death. All the riches I spent my life chasing. I leave them all behind. And my hands? Empty. I came into this world with nothing. I leave it the same."

He was teaching them how to die and showing us how to live.

Legacy isn't about treasure. Titles. Triumphs. It's about *impact*.

Real leaders don't chase gold. They build people up. They don't fear death. They fear a life wasted.

Alexander conquered nations. But in the end, he reminded us:

You don't lead to be remembered. You lead because it matters while you're here.

And here's the part that moves me the most:

His soldiers didn't follow him because they feared him. They followed him because he was one of them.

He bled with them. He slept in the dirt beside them. When water was scarce, he poured his out to show he wouldn't drink if they couldn't.

He knew their names. He carried their burdens. He led them from the front.

That's why his name still echoes. Not because of what he conquered but because of *how* he led.

Alexander commanded his army like a real leader, but he also connected with them. And he showed up—consistently.

Learning Point: Success without health is failure. Titles without impact are hollow. Consistency in the wrong direction doesn't lead to purpose—it leads to burnout.

Be consistent with the things that matter.

With your values. With your health. With your family. With your faith. With your integrity.

Because when your priorities are right consistency becomes a legacy, not a liability.

I want to expand on this idea to share with you what makes teams thrive, schools unite, and leaders stand out?

1. **A Coach Who Shows Up for More Than the Scoreboard:** It's the coach who texts their players the night before a big test, asking if they're ready—not just for the game, but for life. The coach who knows their athletes' dreams off the field, not just their stats. That kind of consistency creates a team that plays for each other, not just the win.
2. **A Principal Who Greets Every Kid by Name:** There's a school I spoke at where the principal stands at the front doors every morning. Rain, snow, doesn't matter—he's out there. He greets every student by name. He fist-bumps the shy ones. He notices when a kid's eyes are a little

heavy. That kind of leadership makes kids feel seen—and when kids feel seen, they show up with purpose.

3. **A CEO Who Checks on Families, Not Just Forecasts:** I met a business leader who starts every Monday meeting asking, "How's your family? How's your heart?" before ever asking about revenue. He created a culture where people work hard—not out of fear, but out of loyalty. They know their leader doesn't just care about the results. He cares about them.

4. **A Teacher Who Refuses to Let a Student Quit:** There's a teacher I'll never forget—she used to pull chairs next to kids who were struggling, not call them out. She stayed after school, on her own time, to tutor a kid who'd already failed two grades. That student graduated because someone believed in him long enough—and consistently enough—to outlast the doubt.

That's the power of presence. That's the influence of consistency. What I learned in war didn't stay in war.

The power of consistency—of showing up, drilling the fundamentals, and leading with discipline—it applies *everywhere.*

In **healthcare**, consistency isn't optional—it's lifesaving.

It's checking vitals twice, not once.

It's washing your hands every single time, even if it's the hundredth patient of the shift.

It's following the protocol when you're tired, understaffed, or emotionally drained—because someone's mother, father, or child is depending on you.

That's what it means to protect someone else's Ohana—their people, their family, their future.

Consistency in healthcare isn't about perfection. It's about showing up strong, even when you don't feel like it, because lives are literally on the line.

In **business**, it's not just one big sales pitch that builds trust. It's the daily grind. The follow-ups. The showing up on time. The honoring your word when nobody's watching.

In **education**, it's not the one great lesson that changes a kid's life. It's the consistent presence. The daily encouragement. The teacher who sees the student every day and says, "I believe in you."

In **marriage**, it's not about flowers once a year. It's about choosing to love every single day. Choosing to stay. Choosing to fight for connection.

In **construction or trucking**, it's not one safe day that matters—it's stringing them together. It's pre-checks. Walk-arounds. Not skipping the "boring" steps.

No matter your uniform—scrubs, steel toes, a suit, or a hoodie—*consistency* is what builds trust, prevents chaos, and drives results.

Consistency

Everyone wants the victory, the spotlight, the applause...

But you only get the results if you do the reps.

In battle, consistency kept me alive. In life, consistency is what keeps me aligned.

Now it's your turn. Consistency doesn't care about fame—it cares about faithfulness. Pick one area of your life, and show up like the world is watching—even when it's not.

Now, here's the final question for this chapter:

Who will you consistently show up for—besides yourself and your family?

Chapter 4

Connection

"The bond that builds teams, families, and futures"

Talent might get you in the door. But connection? That's what keeps you in the room, gets you promoted, and builds your legacy. There's no doubt.

Strong crews are skilled, but they're connected. Connection is what turns individuals into a team, colleagues into collaborators, and strangers into family.

Let's get one thing straight: You can be the most talented person in the room and still fail without connection. Connection is the glue that holds families, teams, marriages, crews, and communities together.

Connection doesn't mean knowing a whole lot of people. It means knowing them deeply, and how well they know you.

I've seen crews on jobsites that have all the skill in the world—but zero communication, zero trust, and zero respect. That's a recipe for disaster. And it doesn't just affect performance—it affects safety, morale, and culture.

In life, connection is protection. When your marriage is struggling, connection brings it back. When your kid is hurting, connection is how they open up. When your team is drifting, connection realigns the mission.

And that is because you can't lead people you don't know. You can't support people who don't feel seen. And you can't win long-term if your crew is disconnected.

In the end, you don't just build success. You build a bond with people. And people build success.

For example, while I was working toward my Family Science and Psychology degrees, I didn't do it alone. I used connection to get across the finish line.

I joined the TRIO program—a service that helps first-generation students figure out the college system. I used Veteran Student Services and Disability Services. I asked questions. I raised my hand. I showed up to the offices that most students walked right past.

I did this because I realized something early: People want to help you—but they can't help you if they don't know you need it.

A lot of students suffer in silence. They sit in the back of the classroom, struggling, hoping somebody notices and reaches out to them.

What they fail to realize is that help isn't hiding, or out of reach. It's waiting for you to go out there and get it. You must speak up. Knock on the door. Get in the room. And if you can't find the room? Build your own. In this situation, it could be starting your own study group.

The world is full of people who want to see you win. Who love to share their knowledge. You just must be willing to connect.

Learning Point: Help is not hiding. It's waiting on your effort, your initiative, and your voice.

Connection turns classrooms into communities. A student who feels connected will try harder, stay longer, and dream bigger. Connection is what turns "I can't" into "I will."

The best teachers do more than teach lessons—they build bridges and connect with their students. A connection with a student today can have a positive effect for decades.

Connections are so powerful that a brown man like me was adopted into a white family—and through the connection of love, that transformed into family. That connection gave me a new community. A new tribe.

If you want a championship, you need the right chemistry, the right connections. But remember it all starts with Choice (Chapter One). Followed by Clarity (Chapter Two). Then Consistency (Chapter Three). But without connection? You won't get there.

Learning Point: Even the best individual talent will lose without collective alignment and deep human connection.

In business, connection turns employees into stakeholders. It's not "their" job—it becomes "our" mission. You don't retain talent with paychecks, you retain it with purpose, culture, and connection.

Connection

Great coaches don't just yell plays—they build trust, because once a player trusts you, they'll run through walls for you.

Any team can high-five when they're winning, but real connection is when they lift each other when they're losing.

You are the salesman of yourself. You've got to connect. Sell who you are. Show your value. Build trust. That's what creates long-lasting relationships and opportunities.

Learning Point: The best opportunities don't always go to the smartest—they go to the most connected. Connection creates access.

I met a guy once who said he wanted to be a speaker. I gave him a shot. At the time, I had no idea he was a wealthy man with some very handy contacts. . But he was grateful for the speaking opportunity, we connected, and he ended up believed in what I was about—and ended up helping me and my cause out by putting my first two books in prisons across the country.

Later, when my wife and I sold two of our rentals, we asked him for advice. That conversation turned into an ice cream franchise. All because of that connection.

When I started my trucking company, I had no clue what I was doing. But Carlos Gomez—the guy selling me the truck—did. So, I said, "I'll buy your truck, but help me get your old route, your DOT number, everything I need." Within a month, I was rolling. And all I had to do was ask! And connect.

Carlos? He got inspired and joined the military. And when I needed help working my way around the trucking world? I called Waylon Pruitt. And Seth Sawls. These men never asked me for anything. They simply led. And because of that, we built a community.

That's the power of connection!

Now let's talk leadership. Leadership has nothing to do with titles or tasks and everything to do with connection. Can the leader reach their team? Can they build trust? Can they unite people when it matters?

Learning Point: You can't lead what you don't love. If you don't care about your people, they won't care about the mission.

When a leader connects, the mission becomes meaningful. And when the mission becomes meaningful, results become unstoppable.

Did you know that people with high EQ (emotional intelligence) are much more likely to win in life—not because they know everything, but because they know how to connect with those around them.

Emotional intelligence is your ability to recognize, understand, and manage your own emotions—and to recognize, understand, and influence the emotions of others. It helps you stay calm under pressure, respond rather than react, and build trust fast.

There are five main areas of emotional intelligence which can really give you an edge for leading:

1. **Self-awareness** – You understand your emotions. You can name what you're feeling and why. You notice how your mood impacts others.
2. **Self-regulation** – You don't fly off the handle. You pause. You manage stress and control your impulses instead of being controlled by them.
3. **Motivation** – You're driven by purpose, not just rewards. You stay positive and keep pushing, even when things get hard.
4. **Empathy** – You can feel what others feel. You listen to understand. You recognize nonverbal cues. You care beyond just the facts.
5. **Social skills** – You know how to communicate, resolve conflict, lead with influence, and build strong relationships.

Think about which of these strengths you already have—and which ones you need to build. Most people are naturally strong in one or two areas, but if you want to lead with connection, you've got to grow in all five.

The good news? Emotional intelligence isn't fixed. You can develop it. Practice it. Strengthen it like a muscle.

And in any industry, relationship, or team—emotional intelligence is a game-changer for connection. Leaders with high emotional intelligence read the room, resolve conflict, and create environments where people feel safe to be real. In any industry, emotional intelligence is a game-changer for connection.

Learning Point: High EQ beats high IQ when it comes to building real teams and lasting success.

IQ, or Intelligence Quotient, is a measure of cognitive ability—how well someone processes information, solves problems, remembers facts, and applies logic. It's often associated with test scores, academic achievement, and mental sharpness.

But being the smartest person in the room doesn't mean you'll be the most successful. IQ might get you the job—but EQ is what helps you keep it, grow in it, and lead others through it.

While IQ measures how smart you are, EQ determines how well you work with others. Sure, a high IQ might impress people. But a high EQ impacts them.

The power of connection also includes having the humility to listen.

I'll be honest with you—I haven't always been the best listener. In fact, if there were an Olympic event for interrupting, I might've taken gold a few times! When someone's speaking, I often catch myself thinking more about what I'm going to say next than hearing what they're saying. That's not connection. That's performance. And connection doesn't live in performance—it lives in presence.

A good listener makes people feel safe, seen, valued and heard. A good communicator doesn't just wait their turn to talk… they lean in to understand. And let me tell you, this is something I'm still working on—every single day.

Connection

Just last week, my wife Elizabeth and I were in the kitchen, having a great conversation our with family. She started speaking, and mid-sentence, I jumped in to add my part. Old habits die hard! I am still trying to break it. But I caught myself. I backed off and reminded myself that listening is leadership. I could see my wife's face change. She didn't have to say a word—her expression said it all. It looked like I had just stepped on her voice, made her feel like what she was saying didn't matter to me. That was never my intention. But that's the thing about connection—it's not just about intent, it's about impact.

When we cut people off, even accidentally, we send a message that says: "What I have to say matters more than what you're saying." It's disrespectful. It's dismissive. It's quite arrogant. And if we're not careful, it becomes a habit that pushes people away—even the ones we love the most.

I love my wife. The last thing I would ever want to do is make her feel unimportant. So, after realizing it, I publicly apologized—not just to make things right with her, but to check myself in front of others. Because if I want to be a better leader, husband, father, friend—I must be a better listener.

How many times do we do that without realizing it? How many times have we unintentionally silenced our spouse, a teammate, an employee, or our own kids?

We've got to slow down. Make space. Pay attention. Because even if we don't mean to hurt someone's feelings, we still can—and often do—just by not being fully aware. And nothing kills connection faster than constantly making someone feel unheard.

Learning Point: check your tone, check your timing, and most of all, check your presence. Don't just hear people. See them. Let them finish. Let them be seen and heard.

When we listen well, certainly prevent conflict, but we also create some wonderful connections. We build trust. We open doors for healing. Listening is, in fact, one of the most powerful ways to lead, love, and lift others. It might be your spouse, your child, your coworker, or a stranger in passing. Every person deserves to feel heard. And you know what else, being listened to just makes others feel great!

If we can get this right in our homes; we'll be better leaders in every other room, we walk into. Real connection doesn't require you to fix everything. It simply requires you to be fully present, heart first, ego last.

We sometimes forget that people love talking about themselves. That's not selfish—it's human. Psychology shows we're wired for it. We know our own stories, our goals, our struggles—so it's easy to talk about ourselves. But emotional intelligence? That's when we slow down enough to hear others. When we master that—we master connection. And we might learn something too, when we listen to others! People have so much wisdom and interesting thoughts to share. Ways of looking at the world differently, that we can learn immensely from.

Things brings me to thinking about what deeper connection is there… than marriage?

Connection

Just this week, I had the honor of officiating the wedding of my wife's younger brother. My brother-in-law. Now, sure—I had the license for this. But more than that, I believed in the love I saw standing before me. It was real. Raw. Rare. And with them, that day, I shared what I call the 5 Cs of a Legendary Marriage.

Let me give you a quick rundown, because honestly—this belongs in more than wedding ceremonies. It belongs in every kind of connection we build in life. Here it is:

The 5 Cs of a Legendary Marriage
1. **Choice** – Love is a decision. Not just once—but daily.
2. **Clarity** – Speak your truth. Be honest. Be clear.
3. **Consistency** – Show up. Keep showing up.
4. **Connection** – Laugh. Touch. Talk. Stay best friends.
5. **Courage** – Be vulnerable. Forgive. Grow together.

These 5 C's build marriages, and they also build teams, families, and friendships. Because connection is the thread that ties us together—and listening is the needle that pulls it through.

Whether you're trying to impress someone during the dating phase... or you're 10 years deep into a commitment... Connection is still king.

And connection—real connection—requires listening. So, I'll keep working on it! And I challenge you to do the same.

If we want to lead, love, and live legendary lives...we can't just speak louder. We've got to listen better.

Lead Like a Legend: The 5 C's That Unlock Greatness

One of my favorite stories on the importance of connection is about a boy named Ryan. Like me, Ryan dreamed of being in the NBA. He lived and breathed basketball—even though he was born with a disability that made everyday movements a challenge. Some kids made fun of him, whispering behind his back and laughing, "What's he doing trying out for basketball? He's handicapped!"

But Ryan had someone in his corner—Mr. Ben, the school principal, a former athlete who now moved through life in a wheelchair. Mr. Ben was that teacher I mentioned earlier, who made it his mission to greet every student at the front doors each morning. No matter the circumstances—he was there.

Every day, he'd smile and call out, "Ryan! Are you trying out for basketball this year?!" He knew Ryan's heart. He knew Ryan had passion. And when tryouts rolled around, Ryan gave it a shot. But sadly… he was cut. Still, Ryan showed up. Every morning. Rebounding balls for the boys' and girls' teams. Helping clean the gym. Supporting from the sidelines. Never complaining.

Then, senior year arrived. Mr. Ben rolled up again and said, "Ryan—you trying out one more time?" Ryan took a deep breath—and said yes. This time, he made the team! But still… he never got to play.

Until one day, one student walked into the coach's office and said, "Coach, Ryan deserves to get in." The coach shook his head. "Not during the playoffs." Then, the team came together. They walked in as one. "Coach, if we're up by fifteen in the fourth quarter… will

Connection

you let Ryan play?" Their coach sighed. Then nodded. "Alright. If that happens—he's in."

It was the final game of the season. The gym was packed, and it was senior night. The team fought harder than ever before—not just to win, but to get Ryan his moment! And finally, in the last minute... the lead hit fifteen. Their coach looked down the bench, smiled, and tapped Ryan on the shoulder. "You're in."

The gym went wild. People held signs. The crowd stood on their feet. They knew what this moment meant.

The other team missed a shot. As the Timberwolves dribbled down the court, the crowd started to chant: "5... 4... 3..." The ball found Ryan's hands. He rose up... fired a deep shot... Buzzer. Swish. The place exploded. Students stormed the court. The football team lifted Ryan onto their shoulders. Mr Ben was crying. So was the coach. So was half the crowd.

Ryan didn't make that shot because he was the best player. He made it because he had teammates who believed in him. A principal who encouraged him. A team that fought for him.

That's the connection. That's community. And isn't that a beautiful thing?

And speaking of community, I want to share something powerful I learned while speaking to healthcare leaders at Intermountain Healthcare. The theme that day was Ohana—that Hawaiian word that means family that I mentioned earlier. It doesn't mean being a blood relative, it's all about the bond and choosing to stand by one another, to lift each other up, and to never let anyone get left behind—or forgotten.

Back to that speaking event. My daughter, Olympia joined me on stage—in full Stitch gear—and helped me bring the message to life. She reminded me, and everyone there, that Ohana is so much more than a word—it's a way of living.

I've had many Ohanas in my life:

- A white family that adopted a brown-skinned kid and loved him like their own.
- A military family that had my back in war.
- A music family who helped me chase the dream.
- A work family in mining, trucking, and teaching.

Ohana means you belong. You matter. You're not alone.

And if you're a leader? You're someone's Ohana! You're someone's safe place. Their anchor. Their answered prayer. What a privilege.

So, don't underestimate the power of showing up. Of knowing names. Of asking, "Are you-okay?"

Learning Point: In a world divided by differences, connection is the revolution.

Something to remember here, too, is that sometimes the best connections are made not by making the last shot or standing on a stage or getting recognition—sometimes the best connections are built by passing the ball and letting others shine.

I think I've drilled the message in by now, but one last reminder: connection does not mean being the loudest voice in the room. It means using your presence to elevate others, noticing who's on the sidelines and pulling them into the game. It's seeing value before the world sees it—and believing in people before they believe in themselves. It's an amazing gift.

Connection is your superpower in leading teams, teaching a class, standing on stage, building a family, or whatever it is you're working on.

Learning Point: If you want to build something legendary—build it on connection. That's how you lead. That's how you last. That's how you leave a legacy.

The Turning Point: Why People Really Change

Before we dive into the final "C" of Legendary Leadership—**Courage**—let's get real.

Most people don't wake up one morning suddenly ready to lead, love, or level up. They don't choose growth because it's trendy or because some motivational quote hit them at the right time on Instagram.

People change when life gives them no other option.

When the pressure mounts, when the pain gets personal, when the comfort zone finally starts to suffocate them.

This is what I call *The Turning Point*—the moment where the discomfort of staying the same becomes greater than the fear of changing.

Through experience, pain, and psychology, we've learned there are **5 core reasons people finally make a change**. Not hype. Not hope. Real, lasting transformation.

These are the reasons people finally fight for something more:

1. Inspiration and Vision

Sometimes, all it takes is a glimpse. A vision of who you could become.

Maybe you see someone doing what you dream of. Maybe you hear a story that makes your excuses sound small.

> **Inspiration opens the door. Vision shows you what's possible.**

When you can see the life that's waiting for you, it starts to pull you forward. It creates movement. Belief. Momentum.

2. Pain and Heartache

Let's not sugarcoat it—**pain is one of the greatest motivators on Earth**.

Breakups. Loss. Rock bottom moments. The betrayal that cuts deep. The failure that haunts you.

Pain gets your attention. It wakes you up. It slaps the comfort out of your hands and demands growth.

> **You can let it break you—or let it build you.**

3. Financial Pressure and Money

Sometimes change isn't philosophical—it's practical.

You're tired of being broke. Of scraping by. Of watching your family go without.

> **Financial pressure can become the fuel that forces you to rise.**

You want to earn more, live more, and give more. That drive can be the spark that starts the fire.

4. Love and Relationships

You'll do things for the people you love that you'd never do for yourself.

> **Love makes you grow. Responsibility makes you rise.**

Whether it's your spouse, your kids, your team, or your community—caring deeply makes you stronger.

When you realize someone else is counting on your leadership, your life starts to shift.

5. Purpose and Faith

At some point, success and motivation aren't enough.

> **You need something deeper—a mission. A reason that doesn't fade when things get hard.**

Faith gives you roots. Purpose gives you wings.

When you believe your story matters, when you know you were created for something more—**you stop playing small**.

Chapter 5

Courage

"It all takes courage"

It takes courage to lead a crew. Courage to rise when life hits hard. It takes courage to say you're sorry. It takes courage to say hello first, to walk away from drama, to speak up about safety, to show emotions, to keep learning and growing.

I don't just talk about courage—I've lived it. And I teach how to bring that same courage to your company culture.

I love the saying that talks about being a dad: You can read books and sing songs about fatherhood—but no lesson hits harder than when the baby is crying in your arms and it's real.

In that moment, you don't need theory. You need a whole lot of courage.

A child's first lessons in courage are not taught—they're witnessed.

Research in developmental psychology supports this. Studies have found that children often model courage based on how they see their caregivers—especially parents—respond to challenges. Fathers tend to model courage by demonstrating physical bravery, taking risks, or standing firm under pressure. Mothers, on the other hand, often model emotional bravery—like showing love through exhaustion, rising after emotional pain, and standing in the fire of daily struggle with grace and grit.

Daughters often learn bravery by watching how their father stands strong, and sons learn it by watching how their mother rises after the fall. But it's the mother who teaches the courage to care deeply, to keep showing up with love after being stretched thin, and to fight battles no one ever sees. Fathers show children how to stand tall. Mothers show them how to stand again. That's just a generalization by the way. Oftentimes, these roles are completely reversed, like a family I know where the father is in the more traditionally famine role and the mother the more traditionally masculine role.

But I digress! What about the kids who don't get that kind of example from either parent? What if the parents aren't around, or worse—model the opposite of courage?

That's real too. And it's why we must be careful who we look up to. From teachers, coaches, mentors, artists, influencers—who we model matters. Because courage, like fear, is contagious.

Even if you didn't get the best example at home, you're not stuck. You're not cursed. In the end, courage is still a choice.

As you've learned already about choice, you can choose to rise. You can choose to break cycles. You can choose to lead with strength, even if you were raised in weakness.

Learning Point: Courage isn't limited to who raised you—it's unleashed by the choices you make next.

Chapter 5

Courage

"It all takes courage"

It takes courage to lead a crew. Courage to rise when life hits hard. It takes courage to say you're sorry. It takes courage to say hello first, to walk away from drama, to speak up about safety, to show emotions, to keep learning and growing.

I don't just talk about courage—I've lived it. And I teach how to bring that same courage to your company culture.

I love the saying that talks about being a dad: You can read books and sing songs about fatherhood—but no lesson hits harder than when the baby is crying in your arms and it's real.

In that moment, you don't need theory. You need a whole lot of courage.

A child's first lessons in courage are not taught—they're witnessed.

Research in developmental psychology supports this. Studies have found that children often model courage based on how they see their caregivers—especially parents—respond to challenges. Fathers tend to model courage by demonstrating physical bravery, taking risks, or standing firm under pressure. Mothers, on the other hand, often model emotional bravery—like showing love through exhaustion, rising after emotional pain, and standing in the fire of daily struggle with grace and grit.

Daughters often learn bravery by watching how their father stands strong, and sons learn it by watching how their mother rises after the fall. But it's the mother who teaches the courage to care deeply, to keep showing up with love after being stretched thin, and to fight battles no one ever sees. Fathers show children how to stand tall. Mothers show them how to stand again. That's just a generalization by the way. Oftentimes, these roles are completely reversed, like a family I know where the father is in the more traditionally famine role and the mother the more traditionally masculine role.

But I digress! What about the kids who don't get that kind of example from either parent? What if the parents aren't around, or worse—model the opposite of courage?

That's real too. And it's why we must be careful who we look up to. From teachers, coaches, mentors, artists, influencers—who we model matters. Because courage, like fear, is contagious.

Even if you didn't get the best example at home, you're not stuck. You're not cursed. In the end, courage is still a choice.

As you've learned already about choice, you can choose to rise. You can choose to break cycles. You can choose to lead with strength, even if you were raised in weakness.

Learning Point: Courage isn't limited to who raised you—it's unleashed by the choices you make next.

Lead Like a Legend: The 5 C's That Unlock Greatness

Everything we've built so far—**Choice, Clarity, Consistency, and Connection**—means nothing without courage. Because knowing the right thing to do means nothing if you're too afraid to do it. Courage is the force that activates the rest, the muscle that pushes your message forward, even when your voice shakes.

Think back to all those outstanding people we mentioned at the start of this book:

- **Martin Luther King Jr.:** didn't just dream—he marched. He stood on the steps of the Lincoln Memorial and said, "I have a dream," even though death threats filled his mailbox.
- **Jesus Christ:** didn't just preach—He picked up His cross. He stepped into betrayal, pain, and sacrifice because His purpose was greater than His fear.
- **Alexander the Great:** didn't just lead armies—he led from the front in a time when kings and generals were expected to fight alongside their men, not command from a tower. He bled with his soldiers. He refused to drink water unless his troops could too.
- **Genghis Khan:** wasn't born powerful. He was abandoned by his tribe. He lived off wild roots and rats. But through unmatched courage, he united warring nations and built an empire.
- **The Buddha:** walked away from luxury, status, and royalty—not to gain more, but to understand suffering and peace.
- **Steve Jobs**: got fired from the company he started and came back to reinvent it.

- **Michael Jordan:** was cut from his high school basketball team—but didn't fold. He practiced like his life depended on it.

They all had one thing in common: **COURAGE.**

They didn't wait for the perfect moment—they moved when it was hard, unpopular, dangerous, or uncertain. And because of their courage, we learned. We benefited. We get to use the freedoms they fought for, the lessons they taught, the technology they sparked. Even **Elon Musk**—whether you like him or not—is pushing the boundaries of what's possible, launching rockets into space and advancing artificial intelligence to carry us into the next era.

These are people who didn't just dream—they had the guts to act.

Which brings me to one of my favorite stories?

The Story of David and Goliath

David was short, under-matched, a shepherd. But he was not a warrior. He didn't have a sword or armor—he had a sling and five smooth stones. The soldiers around him called him foolish, and he didn't have the internet to give him ideas or artificial intelligence or robots to back him up.

But David had something they didn't: *unshakable courage.*

He didn't just step toward the giant—*he ran toward him.* Screaming his name. While everyone else froze in fear, David moved in faith. One boy. One stone. One moment of courage that changed history!

Lead Like a Legend: The 5 C's That Unlock Greatness

The most widely read book throughout history is the Bible, with estimates suggesting over five billion copies sold and distributed worldwide. I bring this up because most of the world's motivational material, speeches, and self-help content borrows from the principles taught in that book.

The Bible says the Philistine army ran after David struck down Goliath. They didn't run when he charged—they ran when they saw their champion fall. David's courage meant he defeated a giant, but he also flipped the momentum of a battle. One boy's bravery ignited a nation's roar.

Learning Point: The courage of one man shook a nation.

So, here's the question I had to ask myself:

What am I running at?

When I started my trucking company, I had no clue what I was doing. But I saw the opportunity and thought, *Oh well—let's go!*

I ran toward it. But what does that mean? I made the calls. I learned what a DOT number was. I got help from Carlos Gomez and others. And I was rolling within a month.

But unlike David, I didn't find a crown on my head.

Back to the military for a moment. I'll never forget that first deployment: 23 of the 32 soldiers in my platoon were hit with IEDs—and many again within the year. Sadly, our leader in our unit was killed. And still—we had to keep going. (The stories of these are in my book, *Conquering Your Colosseum*)

Courage

It took *courage* to get back in a military vehicle after that.

And years later, it took courage to get behind the wheel of a semi-truck again... after being crushed.

Let me tell you what really happened.

A year after I launched the trucking company, after running at it with all I could, I had plans. Big ones. I was going to scale that thing to a million-dollar business and blow everyone's mind with the story: a guy who didn't even have a CDL builds a trucking empire in three years. It was going to be epic.

But life flipped the script. As it usually does.

Yep, twelve months in—it wasn't the company that got crushed. It was me.

I was headed toward Tooele, Utah. The road was clear, then suddenly I came to a dead stop. Traffic slammed to a halt in front of me. I hit the brakes, but I was hauling a full 40-foot container, and if you know trucks... you know that once that momentum builds, it doesn't just stop.

BAM.

Sixty miles per hour. Loaded. And I plowed full force into the back of a stopped semi.

That's when everything changed.

At the hospital I saw people were already posting pictures of the wreck online. Some of the comments said, "No way the driver survived that." Others said, "That's the speaker guy?" "Isn't he supposed to be famous or something?"

Someone wrote: "Why would a public figure be driving a truck?"

The truth? I was grinding in silence but was posting the truck on my Instagram. I was building something with not too much light behind the scenes. I was going to share it when we hit that seven-figure mark. But before I could go viral with my success... I went viral for my survival.

We had just dropped over $40,000 into the truck—it had a new engine, transmission and clutch. Insurance covered the truck—but not the new motor. My wife and I had to eat that cost. No refunds. Just wreckage. Just another hill to climb... Nothing comes easy.

That truck was beautiful—blacked out with spikes, murdered-out grill... I even put it in my "Small Town" country music video. Now? It looked like a crushed soda can.

The engine was so damaged nothing could be taken off... the cab where the driver sits was pushed in and was facing a 3 o'clock position in the middle of the road.

And me?

I was knocked out cold.

I remember slamming my chest on the steering wheel. I'm not going to say whether I had my seatbelt on or not—I'll just say this: Wear your seatbelt.

Courage

I was unconscious when they pulled me out. But I remember praying before the lights went out.

God, please don't let me die. This can't be real. Please... no.

Then darkness.

I don't remember the rescue, but I remember flashes of it. My wife's face. My daughters, Nixeon and Olympia, running through my mind. Memories. Emotions. Pain. Fear.

When I finally came to, diesel fuel was everywhere. People were yelling. Sirens were screaming. And I thought I was going to catch fire. I tried to move—but I couldn't.

My pelvis was pinned.

The dashboard crushed my lower body, and I couldn't breathe. I couldn't move my legs. My ears were ringing. My head was bleeding and spinning and I thought I was paralyzed.

I prayed again.

God, please... not like this. My family needs me. I've come too far. I have a family to lead, and I don't want to die in a truck.

Then my fingers twitched.

My hand moved.

And finally—I could move a finger.

I cried. Not from the pain—but from the hope. *Thank you God!*

survived that." Others said, "That's the speaker guy?" "Isn't he supposed to be famous or something?"

Someone wrote: "Why would a public figure be driving a truck?"

The truth? I was grinding in silence but was posting the truck on my Instagram. I was building something with not too much light behind the scenes. I was going to share it when we hit that seven-figure mark. But before I could go viral with my success... I went viral for my survival.

We had just dropped over $40,000 into the truck—it had a new engine, transmission and clutch. Insurance covered the truck—but not the new motor. My wife and I had to eat that cost. No refunds. Just wreckage. Just another hill to climb... Nothing comes easy.

That truck was beautiful—blacked out with spikes, murdered-out grill... I even put it in my "Small Town" country music video. Now? It looked like a crushed soda can.

The engine was so damaged nothing could be taken off... the cab where the driver sits was pushed in and was facing a 3 o'clock position in the middle of the road.

And me?

I was knocked out cold.

I remember slamming my chest on the steering wheel. I'm not going to say whether I had my seatbelt on or not—I'll just say this: Wear your seatbelt.

Courage

I was unconscious when they pulled me out. But I remember praying before the lights went out.

God, please don't let me die. This can't be real. Please... no.

Then darkness.

I don't remember the rescue, but I remember flashes of it. My wife's face. My daughters, Nixeon and Olympia, running through my mind. Memories. Emotions. Pain. Fear.

When I finally came to, diesel fuel was everywhere. People were yelling. Sirens were screaming. And I thought I was going to catch fire. I tried to move—but I couldn't.

My pelvis was pinned.

The dashboard crushed my lower body, and I couldn't breathe. I couldn't move my legs. My ears were ringing. My head was bleeding and spinning and I thought I was paralyzed.

I prayed again.

God, please... not like this. My family needs me. I've come too far. I have a family to lead, and I don't want to die in a truck.

Then my fingers twitched.

My hand moved.

And finally—I could move a finger.

I cried. Not from the pain—but from the hope. *Thank you God!*

And let me tell you something crazy...

I'm 5'4" tall, right? That day, I thanked God for it. If I was just a few inches taller, my head would've been crushed. No joke.

If you've seen the photo on the back of this book, you know—I shouldn't be here.

I laid awake every night for weeks, reliving that crash. The BAM. The impact. It triggered my PTSD from combat. I started flashing back to the explosions in Afghanistan. I started hearing the blasts. The screaming. The silence after a blast as soldiers tried to radio to those who had just been blown up.

The comeback was physical, but it was also mental. Emotional. Spiritual.

A few days after the wreck, my wife's aunt—who she was incredibly close to—passed away. She was heartbroken. I was broken. And I was extra sad to have put another burden on her.

My youngest daughter Olympia was crying in the hospital room, not understanding why Daddy couldn't be 100% okay. She was my rock and was very loving through all of this.

That's pain. That's life. That's leadership under pressure. But I knew I had to get up again.

It's been months. I still walk with a limp. My leg still gives out sometimes. My back and neck still scream some nights. I've got nerve damage, black spots in my vision, and along with it a reminder in my body every single day that life is fragile—but I'm not finished.

By the grace of God, no one else was hurt. Just me. And I'll take that any day.

But what happened after the wreck? That's what took real courage.

As I laid in the hospital bed—my wife and daughter at my side—their faces etched into my mind forever...

The question wasn't "why me?"

It was, "What now?"

Getting back on my feet. Getting back in the fight. Getting back to the mission. That took more courage than any stage I've ever stood on.

That's what this chapter is about.

Courage when everything crashes. Courage when no one's watching. Courage to lead, even when you're bleeding. Courage to rise—again.

My wrist was broken, my ribs cracked, and my body was bruised and beaten. My left leg still gives out on me sometimes when I walk. My neck is bulging. My back aches daily—not just from the wreck, but from two tours in Afghanistan and life in fight mode.

In a semi, just like in life, your eyes and head must be on a swivel. You must stay alert. Every move matters.

I know this from coal mining, where a wall can collapse in seconds. I know it from the chemical plant, where one missed safety check could cost lives. I know it from construction, where heavy equipment and tight deadlines demand full focus. I know it from teaching, where emotional fatigue and burnout creep in silently but quickly. I know it from the military, where one wrong step in a combat zone can mean life or death. I know it from leadership, where a single decision can shape the culture of an entire crew. And I know it from transportation, where every second counts and every mile is a test of focus and responsibility.

Sometimes, courage doesn't look like swinging a sword or standing on a stage. Sometimes, it looks like saying one of the hardest words: "No."

Sometimes, courage doesn't look like swinging a sword or standing on a stage. Sometimes, it looks like saying one of the hardest words: "No."

No, I can't do that gig—because I promised my daughter I'd be there.

No, I won't chase that opportunity—because my family needs me more than that paycheck.

No, I'm not fine—because I've been breaking silently and need to talk.

It takes courage to slow down when everyone's speeding up. It takes courage to say, "I don't know." It takes courage to admit you're tired, to ask for help, to walk away from something good, to protect something sacred and to simply say, "No."

Courage

More and more it seems we live in a world that praises hustle but forgets the human. I've learned that if you're not careful, you'll build an empire and lose the very people you were building it for. I've seen it happen and it's a very sad sight to see.

Those moments after my wreck reminded me: the world will move on. The stages, the applause, the opportunities—they'll be there for someone else. But my daughter? My wife? My health? My life?

Those are irreplaceable.

Learning Point: It's not just about bravery in the big moments—it's about courage in the daily ones.

I needed to be courageous enough to say, "No, I don't need to do that because I need to be around for my family."

Your home will be rebuilt. The car you worked so hard to get will be crushed or rusted away in a field somewhere. The jobs you held may not even exist in the future. The titles, the trophies, the promotions—they'll all be forgotten. Even your social media will be nothing but digital dust.

But the way you made people feel. The way you showed up when it mattered. The courage you passed on to your kids. The way you loved your spouse during the hard seasons. What about the conversations you had with someone was about to give up? The time you really listened to someone who needed to be heard. The time you chose integrity over ease.

That's what lives on.

Legacy isn't made in what you build. It's made in *who* you build. A hundred years from now, you won't be remembered for your status, you'll be remembered for your spirit. For your character. For your consistency when no one was watching. For your faith when it would've been easier to quit. For the love you gave when it wasn't deserved. For your courage.

So, don't chase what won't matter a century from now. Live now the way you want to be *remembered* a century from now.

That's why I always tell people:

Write the book.

Start the journal.

Document the journey.

Capture the lessons.

Because pages outlive platforms. Paper doesn't crash. Stories don't glitch.

Do you want your great-great-grandkids to know how their grandma and grandpa really lived? What they fought through? What they stood for? What they learned and wish you to know?

Even writing this right now—I realize I don't truly know my own grandparents. I don't know their heartbreaks. Their prayers. Their defining moments. But imagine if they had left a book… A guide to their life. How they built a marriage that lasted. How they got back up after failure. How they kept their faith through the storm. Even how they stayed beautiful, bold, and blessed through the grind. Seriously—how powerful would that be?

Courage

What a gift. What a treasure. What a legacy to pass down. To learn from people who lived 75, 85, 100 years ago. The blessings. The battle scars. The map of lives.

That's what legacy looks like.

And the truth is... your story only matters when it helps others. Read that again. Your story is only needed when it helps others.

When you think about the best speakers? The best entertainers? The best bosses, coaches, mentors, and leaders? They're not the best because of what they've done or for the big house they live in and fancy cars they drive. They're the best because they've used their story to help others.

Period.

They're the best because they've used their story to help others. Read that one again! Read it ten times if you must or put it somewhere that you can read it daily. This isn't about attention. It's about impact. This isn't about being admired it's about someone hearing your story... and finding the strength not to give up.

So don't be shy with your scars. Don't be silent with your survival. Be generous with your journey. Your story is more than survival, it might be someone else's breakthrough.

So, write the book. Live the message. And leave something others can hold long after you're gone.

So, back to David and Goliath, now I turn the question to you:

Lead Like a Legend: The 5 C's That Unlock Greatness

What giants are YOU running toward? Let's be honest—some of you aren't running toward anything. You're running away! When you and your spouse fight—you bounce. When something goes wrong at work or life—you run to drinking, porn, TV, drugs. Even getting lost in work… it's just another escape, if we're honest with ourselves.

You're not running at the giant—you're running from the pain, the stress, the responsibility. I understand.

Some of you? You're stuck in permanent fight mode. You're always angry. Always yelling. Always looking for a reason to explode or blame someone else for the anger you have inside, for the disappointment, sadness, or frustration you carry. You know that the only way out isn't another rage-fit—it's to stop those self-destructive patterns. Once and for all.

You need to get your butt to the gym. You need to blow off steam in a healthy way. Build a good relationship with your body. Build space into your routine for self-care, reflection, family. Connect with a friend. Reset with your crew.

Courage has nothing to do with shining in one big moment—it's choosing the hard, healthy thing over the easy, destructive one. Every day. Okay, you can have a break and relapse here and there. But consistently choose the right way.

Now, what does courage look like in leadership, in family, in business, and in life?

It's the supervisor who speaks up when safety is skipped. It's the team lead who says, "I was wrong. Let's do better." It's the CEO who cancels expansion to protect their team from burnout. It's the parent who puts down the phone to look their kid in the eye. It's the crew member who refuses to engage in gossip and changes the tone of the room. It's the teacher who walks into the classroom ready to pour out even when they're empty. It's the leader who admits, "I don't know the answer… but I'll find it with you."

Courage in leadership isn't loud—it's loyal.

It's not flashy—it's faithful.

It's not always applauded—but it's always remembered.

Do you want to lead like a legend? Of course, you do! So, start by doing the things that scare you. Have the hard conversations. Make the hard choices. Say what needs to be said. Set the boundaries that need to be set. Live the life you're meant to live—not the one people expect because in the end, people don't follow titles.

They follow courage.

Go on, step forward! Run toward the giant! Take the mic. Make the call. Write the truth. Live the truth.

You don't need to be perfect. You just need to be brave enough to begin. You cannot expect God to bless you if you are too lazy to build.

It takes the 5 Cs to build anything worthwhile. It all starts with Choice and ends with the Courage to keep going.

The enemy doesn't need to stop you from what you're doing—if you're too lazy to do what God called you to do, he's already won. Some people are waiting on God to make us do something… to give us the courage… to help us be consistent. But God is like, "I HAVE ALREADY GIVEN YOU ALL THAT ABILITY!" He's waiting on you to apply it.

Learning Point: You're not waiting on a sign. You're waiting on yourself.

Chapter 6

10 Days

> **"Ten days after every training, most people forget almost everything."**

Psychology says it.

Research proves it.

Real life screams it: Ten days after every training, most people forget almost everything.

Think about that. You spend hours—maybe even days—learning something new. You leave inspired. Fired up. Ready to take on the world. And then ten days later? It's all gone. You're back to the old habits. Back to the comfort zone. Back to the way it was.

Why? Because inspiration fades! Motivation leaks and if you don't do something with what you learn—you lose it. In this chapter, we're going to talk about:

1. Why your brain forgets
2. How to beat the 10-Day Fade
3. And what real leaders do to lock in what matters

Let me hit you with a real moment I was at a private event in Atlanta. It was me, Les Brown, and maybe a dozen others. Les Brown. The legend. The lion. A hero in my life. I'd read his books.

Lead Like a Legend: The 5 C's That Unlock Greatness

Watched his videos, studied his voice, his story, his fire. I'd made it a goal to one day shake his hand—and not just shake it—but to look him in the eye and say: "I am the one." If you know the story, you know that line changed his life. But if you don't, here's the real and raw truth:

Les Brown wasn't born with a silver spoon—he was born with the odds stacked against him. He was born in an abandoned building in Liberty City, Florida. He was a twin and with no father. His mother gave him and his brother up for adoption. They were taken in by a cafeteria worker named Mamie Brown—a woman with no money but a heart big enough to raise legends. In school, Les was labeled "educable mentally retarded." That's how the system defined him. Teachers laughed. The students mocked. And for a while—he believed the lie. Then, his brother went off to fight in Vietnam. Les? He was fighting a war in his own mind—against doubt, against fear, against the label.

But one day, a teacher told him something that flipped his world: "Someone's opinion of you does not have to become your reality." Les chase his dream of becoming a DJ, then a speaker, even when nobody believed in him.

Then came the moment that changed everything. Les was sitting in the audience at a motivational event, still unknown—but burning with potential. The speaker on stage looked out at the crowd and said: "Someone in this room is going to do something great. Someone in this room is going to change the world!" Most people clapped politely and forgot it by morning. But Les? That line hit him like lightning. He chased the speaker down, looked him in the eye and declared:

"I am the one. You were talking about me. I am the one." That wasn't arrogance. That was identity. A mindset shift. A moment of becoming. From that day on, Les Brown spoke like a man on a mission. And today?

He's impacted millions, including me.

So, when I sat next to him years later—sharing a stage, eating lunch, answering questions in front of the room—it was surreal. Then, I looked him in the eyes, shook his hand, and said:

"Les... I am the one."

We laughed. We hugged. We connected. We shared stories—mine of growing up in foster care, losing my mother, not knowing who my real father was...of addiction, homelessness, and bouncing from broken homes to shelters. He told me about his brother who went to war. I told him about my own time in the military. We were two men with two scars, two missions and one burning fire. And you know what hit me most? He was real. My hero was a human being—with pain, passion, and purpose. I wrote everything down from that day. Pages and pages.

And then?

I lost the paper. Worse? I forgot most of what he'd said! Let that sink in. Not because it didn't matter—it did! Not because I wasn't locked in—I was all in. But because the brain is wired to let go of what it doesn't revisit.

Have you ever asked your spouse to remind you of the plans—for the third time this week? Do you ever repeat yourself to your kids, and they look at you like it's the first time they've heard it?

Lead Like a Legend: The 5 C's That Unlock Greatness

Have you ever gone over something with your employees—and the next week, it's like it never happened? It's frustrating! But that's not just forgetfulness. That's biology. Studies show we forget most new information within a week. And by ten days, if it hasn't been reinforced, it's gone.

So how do we fight back against this 10-Day fade? Not with more hype.

You fight it with the 3 D's:

- 👉 Dedication
- 👉 Determination
- 👉 Discipline

Those are the muscles behind the message.

But don't forget the 5 C's either:

Choice. Clarity. Consistency. Connections. Courage.

These are the tracks your train runs on. It's not the only path up the mountain—but a solid one. You can tie your shoes a hundred ways—but if they stay tight, they work.

Learning Point: If you want to remember, you've got to return. If you want to grow, you've got to grind. And if you want change to stick? You've got to live what you learn.

Now, let's talk about how to lock it in. Let's talk about how real leaders turn lessons into legacy. Let's build something that sticks

Let's crush the 10-Day Fade!

Chapter 7

How to Beat the Ten-Day Fade

"Lock it in and beat it!"

If you don't want to forget... If you don't want to fall back into old patterns... If you want to change your life and lead like a legend, you've got to fight for what you've learned.

Here are 5 proven ways to lock it in and beat the 10-Day Fade:

1. Review Within 24 Hours

Your brain starts dumping information almost immediately. So don't wait a week to revisit it.

Pro tip:

Within 24 hours, write down what stood out. Review your notes. Speak it out loud. Ask yourself: "What am I supposed to do with this?" Don't just read it. Engage it.

2. Teach It to Someone Else

You never fully learn a thing until you teach it.

Find someone—your spouse, your kid, your team—and share the key takeaways. Teaching forces your brain to organize, simplify, and retain information.

Pro tip:

Ask yourself, "If I had to teach this in 60 seconds, what would I say?"

Boom. Locked in!

3. Anchor It to an Action

Knowledge without action is just potential. You've got to move on it.

Example:

You heard a message on gratitude.

Start sending one thank-you text a day.

You heard a training on leadership.

Schedule a one-on-one with someone on your team.

Tie what you learned to a real, visible action—because action is memory's best friend.

4. Repeat. Revisit. Reignite.

You don't brush your teeth once and say, "Cool, I'm good for life."

It's the same with learning.

Build a system:
- Set a reminder to review key notes weekly
- Record a voice memo of your own takeaways

- Put quotes or takeaways on sticky notes or your phone lock screen

The message that gets repeated… becomes remembered.

5. Connect It to Your Story

This is a game-changer.

If you want something to stick, tie it to who you are.

Ask yourself:

"How does this apply to my life?"

"Where have I seen this before?"

"How can this help someone I love?"

When a lesson becomes personal, it becomes permanent.

Let's not forget—I'm not talking here about remembering more… I'm talking about becoming more.

I'm sure you've heard, "Knowledge is power."

Nah. That's only half the story!

"Applied knowledge is power."

If you want to beat the fade, you've got to work the word, not just hear it. You've got to build rituals, not just chase results. And you've got to train your mind like a soldier train for battle—every single day.

Ask yourself this:

What's something powerful you learned in the last 10 days?

Did you apply it?

Or did you let it fade?

Let's fix that right now.

Remember:

Studies show we forget up to **70% of new information within 24 hours**, **90% by day 10**, and up to **98% by day 14**—unless we review and apply it. Don't just read this chapter. **Revisit it. Teach it. Use it.** That's how you beat the fade and become the kind of leader who remembers what matters.

Chapter 8

What Real Leaders Do Differently

> "Leaders don't just receive information — they build transformation.

"We've all forgotten things at work. We've all missed details. We've all told someone something three times and they still didn't do it. We've been that person, too nodding during training, then drawing a blank the next day.

Forgetfulness isn't the problem. Lack of reinforcement is. And that's where leadership shows up because leaders don't just receive information — they build transformation. That's the difference. Anybody can listen to a podcast, sit in a meeting, or attend a workshop.

But leaders ask:

"How can I use this to make my team better?"

"How do I make sure these sticks?"

"How can I turn this into culture, not just content?"

Have you ever given your team clear instructions, and a week later—crickets? Have you ever been in a meeting where everyone nods... but no one follows through? I'm sure you're beginning to see here that it's not because they didn't care. It's because you didn't build the bridge between knowledge and action.

Here's what legendary leaders do it:

They simplify the message.

- Clear beats clever.
- If your team can't repeat it, they won't remember it.
- They revisit the mission constantly.
- Repetition isn't annoying — it's necessary.
- People don't need new messages every week. They need the right one, driven deep.

They lead by example.

- If you're not living what you teach, no one's following.
- You want people to remember the mission? Be the mission.

They give room for repetition, practice, and reflection.

- Learning isn't a one-time shot — it's a lifestyle.
- They don't assume—they check for understanding.
- Ask: "What did you take from that?"
- "How would you explain it to someone else?"
- That's where the gold is.

If you're a leader — of a team, a family, a classroom, a company, or your own life — here's the truth: You can't afford to forget what matters because if you forget, they forget. If you drop the message, they drop the mission.

What Real Leaders Do Differently

Leadership means carrying the weight of vision when others are tired repeating the right message when others are distracted...and showing what it looks like to stay disciplined long after the feeling fades.

Let me bring it full circle:

The 10-Day Fade is real. But it's not the end — it's just the test. It's the gap between inspiration and implementation. And the leaders who close that gap? They don't just remember the message, they become the message.

So, here's the challenge: Before you turn the page, choose one thing you've learned in the last ten days — from this book, from life, from experience — and anchor it.

Write it down. Teach it. Practice it. Build it into who you are.

Learning Point: The world doesn't need more people who have heard a good message. The world needs leaders who live it.

Chapter 9

Be the One

> **"Be the leader in you rising!"**

You made it this far for a reason. You didn't just skim pages. You didn't just flip through the stories. You showed up. You leaned in. You felt something wake up inside you. That "something"? It's the leader inside you rising! I hope by now you're seeing that this isn't just a book about leadership. This is about living legendary. It's not about being perfect. It's not about having a title. It's not about what's in your bank account or how many followers you've got.

It's about how you show up when life hits. It's about who you are when nobody's clapping. It's about the choices you make, the clarity you build, the consistency you commit to, the connections you grow, and the courage you bring when it's hard to breathe.

Let me remind you of something: Every principle in this book—every tool, every lesson, every firestorm you walked through—was designed to activate something in you.

You've been given:

The 5 Cs of Legendary Leadership:

1. **Choice:** You own your path.

2. **Clarity:** You know your mission.
3. **Consistency:** You show up daily.
4. **Connections:** You lead with heart.
5. **Courage:** You rise even when it hurts.

The 3 D's of Discipline:

1. Dedication.
2. Determination.
3. Discipline.

These aren't buzzwords, they're you're battle tools! You've also learned how to defeat the 10-Day Fade, and you've heard stories of Les Brown, of my own journey, of turning pain into purpose. You're on your way!

Now?

It's your turn.

There's a moment in every great story where the hero stops waiting to be rescued… and decides to become the rescuer.

This is that moment.

This is where you stop waiting for someone to hand you a title, a break, or a permission slip. This is where you say, "I am the one." I'm not saying it'll be easy. I'm saying it's possible because leaders aren't born—they're built. And you, my friend, have been building every step of the way.

Now, here's the final challenge:

Don't let this book sit on a shelf.

Don't let it become one of those things you read, got pumped up about… and forgot tendays later. *Do* something with it.

Teach the 5 Cs to your team.

Practice the 3 Ds in your home.

Tell your story with courage and vulnerability.

Choose to lead—even when it's messy.

Learning Point: Your legacy isn't built in a single moment—it's built in every decision you make from this moment on.

Be the one who remembers. Be the one who leads. Be the one who changes the game.

You weren't just meant to read this book… You were meant to live it.

To Lead Like a Legend!

But before we close this thing out, I need to tell you a story.

When I was in the military, there was a drill sergeant who had a saying that burned into my brain "Standards start in the dark." He meant that the first standard you set every day happens before anyone even sees you. Before your boss sees you. Before your family talks to you. Before your team counts on you. It starts the second you open your eyes.

Winning doesn't start at work.

Be the One

Winning doesn't start when you get recognition.

Winning starts before the world even knows you're awake.

I'll never forget one morning—basic training, Fort Benning, Georgia. It was 4:30 AM. Pitch black. I was exhausted. I had blisters on my feet. My shoulders torn up from ruck marches, and every muscle in my body begged to stay in bed.

But I had a choice. That first second when my eyes cracked open. That was the real battleground. I could hit snooze mentally.

Or I could fight! I threw off the blanket like it owed me money. I put my boots on and squared my uniform squared away. The barracks were spotless, my gear ready and I didn't wait for the drill sergeant to scream.

I led myself before anyone else could. Most people rolled out of bed half-asleep and half-committed. But not the ones who made it. Not the ones who became legends, because standards set the tone. And once you drop your standard first thing in the morning—you will drop it all day long.

Here's your new mindset:

You don't win the day at noon. You win it the moment your alarm goes off. That first thought? That first choice? That's where you separate being average from being legendary. Leaders lead themselves before they lead anyone else. Champions rise when no one's watching. Legends are forged in the decisions nobody applauds. It's easy to say you want it when the sun's up and the coffee's brewed. It's a whole different beast to want it when it's dark, cold, and nobody's watching.

And that's what I'm challenging you to do:

Be the one who rises when it's easier to sleep.

Be the one who polishes their armor when no one else even shows up to the fight.

Be the one who keeps their standards high—because your life depends on it.

The world isn't short on critics. It's not short on people who can point fingers, complain, or quit. It's short on leaders. Real ones. Built ones. Legendary ones.

So be the one. Be the spark in a dark world. Be the hand that lifts. Be the voice that steadies. Be the fighter who stays standing when others sit down. And when your story is told—because it will be told—

let them say you choose wisely, lived courageously, loved deeply, and led like a legend.

This isn't just motivation. It's a mission. Now, get out there! Live it. Bleed it. Build it.

Lead Like a Legend.

Chapter 10

Rise, Champion

"Learn to lead yourself"

In order to be a great leader, you must first learn to lead yourself. Period. Because a broken leader can't build anything whole. A broken leader creates confusion, mistrust, and pain in others—not out of intention, but because they never healed what's within.

So yes—it matters if you're struggling with anxiety, depression, grief, loss of a loved one, financial pressure, insecurity, addiction, burnout, or trauma., because what's inside of you eventually spills out.

But here's the truth: You can overcome those things.

It starts with a choice, then your thoughts turn into actions and your actions shape your life, (and the lives of others). So go ahead—be that "wannabe." You must believe change is possible. You have to believe that a better version of you is within reach. Because it is.

Your victory... your leadership... will become someone else's success story. I'm speaking directly to you—the one holding this book. You are a good mother. You are a good father. Sibling.

Lead Like a Legend: The 5 C's That Unlock Greatness

Warrior. Champion. You may have been the underdog but listen—we are all underdogs.

And yet... we rise.

It's a tug of war between you and life. But you can win.

Do yourself a favor do yoga, or the gym or go for a run. Work through the pain. Burn the fat—and the lies in your head while you're at it. Look and feel like a warrior so that when you walk into a room, people feel it.

They'll treat you differently. Not because you said something amazing—but because they can see your discipline. They can feel your dedication. Your determination will speak for you. You can't buy a championship. You can't buy a work ethic. You can't purchase a six-pack. It's built with blood, sweat, and tears. It's the only way.

They say only one in every 25,000 adults has visible abs! So what? You can be that one. You want to rise? Invest in yourself. Only 23.5% of the U.S. population over 25 holds a bachelor's degree. You want in? Go get it. I failed four times. I had a 1.3 GPA. But like I've said before: It's not over until I win. Want to go even higher? In 2025, only 14.4% of U.S. adults hold a master's degree. How about higher? Less than 3.3% have a doctorate.

Be the first. Be the one.

Why? Because investing in yourself is the best thing you can ever do. It's true—you don't need a traditional degree to succeed. But the title of education still holds weight in the business world.

A lot of people say, "I'll just start and run a business myself." And that's great—we need more dreamers. But here's the truth most won't tell you: Words are easy. Actions are true. Everybody talks about being an entrepreneur. Everybody posts motivational quotes and says they're building an empire. But statistically?

Most people don't.

Most people won't.

Most people quit.

According to the U.S. Census and Small Business Administration, about 10% of Americans own a business. Out of 335 million people, that's only around 33 million business owners. And of those? Only a fraction run their business full-time—or profitably. Let me say that louder: Being your own boss sounds exciting... but most people never take the first real step. That's the gap between talking and leading. That's the difference between a goal and a grind.

You want to start a business? Then start one. You want to lead others? Then lead yourself first. You want to win in the marketplace? Then train like a champion—every single day.

Ownership isn't about a logo or an LLC. It's about ownership of your habits. Your decisions. Your mornings. Your mindset. Your mission.

Did you know that most people don't fail because of competition. They fail because of comfort. Comfort is the silent killer of champions. So, no—entrepreneurship isn't your easy way out.

Lead Like a Legend: The 5 C's That Unlock Greatness

It's your hard way into everything you were born to be. And I'm not here to pat your back. I'm here to push you forward.

If you want to rise, then rise above the average. Rise above the excuses. Rise above the 90% who just talk. Be the one out of ten who builds something. As an author, speaker, and musician, I'm telling you—life is competitive. You can settle. Or you can rise.

In the chemical plant, the military, the coal mine—they all respected the ones who showed up with the papers. Yes, experience is golden. But sometimes you must set your pride down and level up. Education is one of the best investments you can make. And that's coming from someone who already has six figures, a few businesses, and a bestselling book and a few music awards.

You know what that degree showed? It showed that I showed up. It showed I conquered what most people don't finish. You can't take money with you when you go. You can't take titles or fame. But your knowledge, your skillset, your impact? That lives on.

So why aren't you out there being the best version of you? Is it laziness? A lack motivation. Be honest with yourself.

I was a homeless child… a drug addict… a foster kid. I graduated high school as homecoming king. I lost my mom to suicide. I ended up homeless again—because of my own choices. I've been sued, jailed eight times… you name it.

My story is full of rock bottoms and restarts. I went to war—twice. I begged my wife not to leave me because I was acting like a fool. I was in a car with a plan—a plan to end my life. Even after

Rise, Champion

attending suicide prevention training in the military... I didn't know what else to do. I was ready to give up.

I crushed my hand in the coal mines. Had multiple surgeries. I've had other work-related injuries. I was nearly killed in that semi crash—an injury that still affects me today and will for the rest of my life.

And yet—I changed. It wasn't easy.

But change was hard-earned... and real. I get up every day and lift ten to twenty pounds—because that's what the doctor said I can do. But when you see me, you'll see it: I look like a warrior. There will never be a question.

I am God's child—and I represent Him. Your family needs you. Your coworkers need you. Your community needs you.

You never know when your words or your compliment might save someone's life—because they're right there on the edge, getting beat down by life. People are really struggling. I hear it every time I speak. Children, adults, in tears. Many are at the end of their rope.

Where are you at, my friend?

So, rise, Champion.

Be the legendary leader.

Be the hero.

Let's build an army of leaders together!

Lead Like a Legend: The 5 C's That Unlock Greatness

You can find my words in music videos, books, and audiobooks. But I want to reach classrooms, boardrooms, locker rooms, and the ends of the earth. Why?

Because when I was a boy, I remember sitting in a bathtub, scrubbing my skin raw. I didn't know who I was. I had just been adopted by a white family, and my little heart was crushed. I scrubbed and scrubbed, wishing I could scrub the brown off my skin... But one day, a motivational speaker came to my school. He said we could be heroes. Kids like me! Twenty-seven years later, I stood in that same school district... on that same stage... behind the same piano... with the mic in my hand. And I told those kids:

You can be a hero. We charge toward the giants in our lives. We call them out by name. Because our insecurities are steppingstones toward what God has called us to do.

So, fight on! Help your classmates. Help your family. Help your coworkers, your friends, and your community.

This is your moment.

To every father and every mother...To every student grinding through school, unsure if they're enough...To every soldier, every teacher, every nurse, every janitor, coach, CEO, cashier, and coal miner...To the leaders in warehouses and on the battlefield... in classrooms, courtrooms, and correctional facilities...To the truckers, entrepreneurs, construction crews, counselors, pastors, and police officers...To the tired, the tested, and the overlooked—this book was written for you.

Rise, Champion

You matter. Your work matters. Your story matters. Your leadership matters.

Whether you're behind a desk or behind a plow... in the streets or on the stage... this world needs your voice, your strength and your courage. So, whatever you do, wherever you are...

Rise, Champion.

Chapter 11

Letter to Self

"Write it. Right here. Right now!"

Can remember when back to when you were eight years old—what did you want to be when you grew up?

I'll go first. I wanted to be in the NBA. A Ninja Turtle. A cowboy, especially when I had my cowboy boots on. I was wild, creative, full of energy and dreams that had no limit. By the time I was eleven or twelve, I thought being rich and, in the military, would be the ultimate combo. Like G.I. Joe with a Lamborghini! But if I could write myself a letter, and have that twelve-year-old version of me read it, it would go something like this:

Dear Young Ryan,

You will make it. Not overnight. Not with ease. But you'll make it.

Think of it like picking up weights, you grow slow. You get stronger little by little. Some days you'll wonder if it's even working… but I promise you, it is. There's no such thing as fast success unless someone drops a check in your lap or hands you a trust fund. And even then? If you don't have the wisdom and education to make that money grow, you'll spend it like a lottery winner and end up broke and confused before the ink dries.

Letter to Self

So, here's the truth: Bet on YOU.

Ryan books are gold! Read books. Not just for school—for your soul, for your future.

Please read: "Can't Hurt Me" by David Goggins

READ Mike Tyson, "Undisputed Truth"

READ "As a Man Thinketh" by James Allen

READ "Homeless to Billionaire" by Andres Pira

READ "Rich Dad, Poor Dad" by Robert Kiyosaki

Listen to podcasts that stretch your mind. People like Ed Mylett, Eric Thomas, Inky Johnson. Surround yourself with voices that make you rise.

And when you run? Run like you've got an army behind you~ Fight for your future. Don't wait for someone to save you—be your own rescue mission. And do what you wish for. Because the dream God placed in your heart isn't random. It's a calling.

Now, to the reader holding this book...

If you could go back and speak to your younger self—what would you say? Would you tell yourself to take that chance?

To walk away from that toxic relationship? To stop doubting your worth? To apologize? To dream bigger? To forgive yourself?

Write it. Right here. Right now!

Lead Like a Legend: The 5 C's That Unlock Greatness

(Insert blank journaling pages here – 2 to 4 pages)

Now, it's your turn to write a letter to yourselves. What does your younger self need to hear? What did they deserve to know? What truth, what love, what strength would you pour into them?

(Insert blank journaling pages here – 2 to 4 pages

Now that you've revisited your younger self… let's fast forward.

You're seventy-five years old, sitting on a porch in your rocking chair, with wisdom in your wrinkles. If you could go back in time to right now—to today—what would you tell yourself?

Would you say, "Go all in", "Love harder", "Slow down and savor this moment" or "Stop being scared and go for it" Would you say, "Make the call, forgive the past, chase the dream"? If you could time-travel back to the version of you holding this book… what advice would your older self-give you?

Think about that.

Then act on it.

The gap between where you are and where you want to be is filled with the steps you're scared to take. But our future self is already cheering for you. Now it's your move.

Let's go!

If you haven't already, it's so important to write your dreams and goals down. If you don't—you will forget. And when you forget, that's it. Like the wind passing through the plains of the earth,

Letter to Self

your legend will drift the same way. Do it for you. Do it for your kids. Do it for those whom you will one day inspire. Do it for that special person in the rocking chair.

You have a story. We all have a story. Now use it (and the 5 C's!) to better the lives of others.

Goodbye, my friends. I'll see you on the battlefield of life!

Bonus Chapter

Fuel for the Fight — Quotes to Lead, Rise, and Dominate

"Quick Hits of Motivation When You Don't Have Time to Read a Whole Chapter"

I get it, sometimes you don't have time to read a full chapter, but you still need that fire. You need fuel. And you don't want to fall into the trap of the ten-day fade. Good!

For me, quotes to the trick. One good line can flip my mindset, shift my spirit, and get me back in the fight. So here it is—one hundred quotes broken into fast-access sections for whatever kind of moment you're in:

- When you need discipline
- When you feel beat down
- When you're trying to lead
- When you need to remember God's got you
- When you're ready to go beast mode

This chapter's your personal ammo box. Flip to it, find your fire, and get back in the game.

ERIC THOMAS (ET THE HIP HOP PREACHER)

Eric was homeless. Eating out of trash cans. Sleeping in abandoned buildings. And now? He's one of the highest-paid motivational speakers in the world.

Eric Thomas didn't just talk about pain—he absolutely lived it. He was abandoned by his father, dropped out of high school, lived on the streets of Detroit... he had every excuse to quit. But he found purpose through faith and grind. He got up every day and made a decision: "I'm not staying here."

He walked into a church one day, not looking for a sermon, but for shelter. He ended up finding both. That moment sparked a fire that never went out. He went back to school. Got his GED. Then a bachelor. Then a master. Then a Ph.D. And all along the way, he kept speaking. Kept pouring into others the fire he had to build from nothing. ET's greatness didn't come from talent. It came from choosing pain over pity and purpose over comfort. Every. Single. Day.

Quotes from ET:

"When you want to succeed as bad as you want to breathe, then you'll be successful."

"Don't make a habit out of choosing what feels good over what's actually good for you."

"Everybody wants to be a beast, until it's time to do what beasts do."

"Some of you love sleep more than you love success."

"You're not failing. You're forming."

"Pain is temporary. Quitting lasts forever."

"I can. I will. I must."

"Be phenomenal or be forgotten."

"You will not outwork me."

"Average skill with phenomenal will."

"ET didn't wait for the fire—he became it. So can you." — Ryan Stream

LES BROWN

Les was labeled "educable mentally retarded" in grade school. He grew up on the floor of an abandoned building and gave motivational speeches to empty chairs when no one would book him. And still—he rose.

Les Brown is proof that the opinions of others don't define you unless you let them. Adopted as a baby, overlooked in classrooms, and told he wouldn't make it, but still, he refused to be boxed in by labels. With a passion for speaking and a voice that carried conviction, Les fought for every opportunity to speak. He spoke at schools, in prisons, on the streets, anywhere someone would listen.

One day, someone did. And the world hasn't stopped listening since!

Fuel for the Fight — Quotes to Lead, Rise, and Dominate

Les believed that greatness wasn't something you were born with, that it was something inside you, waiting to be called out.

Les's life didn't come wrapped in inspiration. He had to dig it out of the dirt and in doing so, he showed the world that dreams don't have expiration dates.

Quotes from Les Brown:

"It's not over until I win."

"Shoot for the moon. Even if you miss, you'll land among the stars."

"Too many of us are not living our dreams because we are living our fears."

"You don't have to be great to get started, but you have to get started to be great."

"Other people's opinion of you does not have to become your reality."

"Ask for help. Not because you're weak, but because you want to remain strong."

"No matter how bad it is… or how bad it gets… I'm going to make it!"

"You were born to win, but to be a winner, you must plan to win, prepare to win, and expect to win."

"Align yourself with people that are going places."

"You have greatness within you."

"When Les said, 'You've got greatness within you,' he meant it. So, believe it." — Ryan Stream

MARCUS AURELIUS (THE STOIC EMPEROR)

Marcus Aurelius ruled the Roman Empire, but never let power rule him. While other emperors drowned in their egos, Marcus Aurelius battled with himself. Not with swords and shields but with thoughts and temptations. He fought to remain grounded, wise, and just in a world full of noise.

He journaled at night—not to impress anyone, but to remind himself who he was striving to become. That journal became "Meditations", a timeless treasure chest of Stoic wisdom that's still guiding leaders, warriors, and dreamers nearly two thousand years later.

But what makes Marcus powerful is the fact that he lived those quotes that he wrote. In times of plague, war, betrayal, and grief, he kept his compass steady.

His legacy wasn't built on conquering land, but on mastering the self.

Quotes from Marcus Aurelius:

"You have power over your mind—not outside events. Realize this, and you will find strength."

"Waste no more time arguing what a good man should be. Be one."

"The impediment to action advances action. What stands in the way becomes the way."

"If it is not right, do not do it. If it is not true, do not say it."

"Dwell on the beauty of life. Watch the stars and see yourself running with them."

"The best revenge is not to be like your enemy."

"Choose not to be harmed—and you won't feel harmed."

"Our life is what our thoughts make it."

"Death smiles at us all. All a man can do is smile back."

"Look well into yourself; there is a source of strength which will always spring up."

"He ruled the world, but he ruled himself first. That's power." — Ryan Stream

KOBE BRYANT (THE BLACK MAMBA)

Kobe wasn't supposed to be the next big thing. He was the kid who skipped college, the kid from Italy, the one with the famous dad and a target on his back. They doubted him. Said he was selfish. Said he wasn't ready. But Kobe never listened to the noise, he listened to the inner voice that whispered, "Work harder."

Kobe lived in the gym. He'd show up at 4 a.m. for practice, run drills for hours, obsess over his footwork like it was a chess game. He'd shoot one thousand shots a day, study films while others partied, and train like he had no talent. Because for him? Obsession was the difference between talent and greatness.

In 2013, at age 34, Kobe tore his Achilles tendon. Most players would've crumpled. He didn't. He walked to the free throw line, on a torn Achilles, and drained both shots. Then he walked off the court like a warrior.

His pain didn't define him. His response did.

When he retired, he didn't relax or lose himself he reinvented himself. He wrote children's books, he won an Oscar, mentored young athletes. And he loved his daughters fiercely. Kobe did more than play the game of basketball—he played the game of life like every moment mattered,

The Mamba Mentality wasn't about basketball, it was about excellence, ownership, and obsession with becoming your best. No excuses. Just work.

Quotes from Kobe Bryant:

"The moment you give up is the moment you let someone else win."

"Everything negative—pressure, challenges—is all an opportunity for me to rise."

"Dedication sees dreams come true."

"I don't want to be the next Michael Jordan. I only want to be Kobe Bryant."

Fuel for the Fight — Quotes to Lead, Rise, and Dominate

"Great things come from hard work and perseverance. No excuses."

"I'll do whatever it takes to win games, whether it's sitting on a bench waving a towel, handing a cup of water to a teammate, or hitting the game-winning shot."

"Once you know what failure feels like, determination chases success."

"If you're afraid to fail, then you're probably going to fail."

"The beauty in being blessed with talent is rising above doubters to create a beautiful moment."

"Rest at the end, not in the middle."

"Kobe didn't wait for motivation. He hunted it. And then he hunted greatness." — Ryan Stream

CAITLIN CLARK

Have you seen this girl showing up all over ESPN, SportsCenter, and your social feed? She's not just a shooter—she's a shot maker, a record breaker, and a culture changer.

From the moment she stepped onto the court at the University of Iowa, Caitlin didn't just want to play basketball—she wanted to raise the standard. She put in the extra shots. She studied the game. She stayed late. She demanded more from herself—and then pulled her team up with her.

She didn't just lead the NCAA in points. She led her teammates to packed arenas, national attention, and brand-new belief. Girls who never had a crowd suddenly had fans, interviews, and TV deals. And Caitlin? She didn't hoard the spotlight—she brought the whole squad with her. That's what true leaders do. They don't just win. They build a winning culture.

She proved that greatness isn't about ego or stats—it's about showing up every day, getting better, and bringing others with you. That's why Iowa became must-watch TV. That's why the WNBA is exploding with energy and fans. Because Caitlin Clark made people care—not just about her, but about the mission.

MICHAEL JORDAN

Michael was cut from his high school team and constantly overlooked. But Michael Jordan didn't let that bother him, he calculated, and he went to work. He built the most dangerous mentality in sports: I'll prove you wrong... and I'll never stop.

Michael became the greatest of all time not just because of what he could do with a basketball, but because of what he could do with failure. He used it, and he fueled himself with it.

Jordan wasn't just playing a game—he was playing for the legacy. For every kid who was ever told they weren't good enough.

MJ turned pressure into poetry, setbacks into showtime. He didn't chase greatness; he made greatness chase him.

Quotes from Michael Jordan:

Fuel for the Fight — Quotes to Lead, Rise, and Dominate

"I've failed over and over and over again in my life. And that is why I succeed."

"Some people want it to happen, some wish it would happen, others make it happen."

"Never say never, because limits, like fears, are often just an illusion."

"Earn your leadership every day."

"You must expect great things of yourself before you can do them."

"Talent wins games, but teamwork and intelligence win championships."

"I can accept failure; everyone fails at something. But I can't accept not trying."

"Heart is what separates the good from the great."

"Always turn a negative situation into a positive situation."

"If you quit once, it becomes a habit. Never quit!"

"Jordan did more than raise the bar—he became it." — Ryan Stream

INKY JOHNSON

Inky was on the path to the NFL, a rising star at Tennessee. Then, one hit changed everything. Inky Johnson suffered a life-altering injury that paralyzed his right arm and took his football dreams off the table.

But that's not where his story ends. That's where it began.

Instead of sinking into bitterness, Inky rose into purpose. He realized his platform wasn't his sport, it was his story. And what the world needed wasn't another athlete. It needed a voice that understood pain but chose purpose anyway.

Inky's story proves your circumstance doesn't define you, your character does.

Quotes from Inky Johnson:

"Perspective drives performance every day of the week."

"Commitment is staying true to what you said you would do, long after the mood has left you."

"The process is more important than the product."

"Don't just go through it. Grow through it."

"Character supersedes circumstance."

"People don't burn out because of what they do. They burn out because life makes them forget why they do it."

"Tough times reveal character."

"Your why must be deeper than your pain."

"Every day I'm trying to be the best version of myself."

"Inky's arm stopped moving, but his mission never did." — Ryan Stream

ANNA BISSELL - The First Female CEO Who Outlasted the System

In 1889, Anna Bissell did something unheard of. Her husband—Melville Bissell—had just passed away, leaving behind five children and a small company that made carpet sweepers. In a world where women couldn't vote, couldn't open a business account, and weren't taken seriously in boardrooms, everyone assumed the business would be handed off to a man. But Anna didn't wait for permission. She stepped in. She took the reins. And she became the first female CEO in American history.

She wasn't handed a golden ticket. She was handed a family, a funeral, and a failing company—and she turned it into a global empire. She studied every part of the business. She defended her patents in court. She took Bissell international. And while she built the brand, she also built people—offering worker pensions and fair wages long before it was the "right thing to do."

Anna didn't have social media. She didn't have a business degree. She had relentless consistency—a commitment to show up, speak up, and lead with compassion and strategy, day after day. That's the kind of leadership that doesn't just break ceilings—it builds foundations.

Legendary Leadership Lesson: You don't have to be born into a legacy to build one. You don't need status or spotlight to lead. Consistency is louder than connections.

When the world says, "Step aside," Step in. Show up. Outlast the system.

GENGHIS KHAN

Genghis was feared. He was ruthless. He was brilliant. But most of all, he was unstoppable. Born into tribal exile, Genghis Khan clawed his way through betrayal, starvation, and war to become the greatest conqueror the world has ever seen.

He didn't inherit power. He earned it through resilience, loyalty, and brutal lessons. He turned rival tribes into a single force. He led with strategy, not just strength. And when the world doubted him, he rode harder.

Genghis Khan didn't conquer with numbers. He conquered with mindset. And that's what still lives on.

Quotes from Genghis Khan:

"If you're afraid – don't do it. If you're doing it – don't be afraid."

"Conquering the world on horseback is easy; it is dismounting and governing that is hard."

"It is not sufficient that I succeed—everyone else must fail."

"A leader can never be happy until his people are happy."

"An action committed in anger is an action doomed to failure."

"The greatest happiness is to scatter your enemy and drive him before you."

"Without the vision of a goal, a man cannot manage his own life, much less the lives of others."

"Even the greatest warriors make mistakes."

"The strength of a wall is neither greater nor less than the courage of the men who defend it."

"Who can't stop a storm must learn to ride it."

"He started with nothing, built everything, and ruled without permission." —Ryan Stream

STEPH CURRY – The Sharpshooter Nobody Believed In

You'd think being the son of an NBA player would open all the doors. But for Steph Curry? Every door slammed in his face.

He was too small. Too scrawny. His shot was weird. The big schools didn't want him. Duke said no. UNC said no. He ended up at Davidson, a tiny school no one talked about. And all he did? Light up the NCAA Tournament and drop 30+ on NBA-level defenders.

But still, when he entered the league, scouts doubted him. They said he'd get bullied, that his ankles were too weak. That he'd never last. Some coaches even thought he should be traded early in his career.

But Steph didn't listen to critics, he listened to his work ethic, his faith, and his fire. He practiced shots from deep before anyone else dared. He trained like a sniper. And he kept smiling while he burned every doubt to the ground.

Now? He changed the entire game. He turned the three-point shot into a weapon of mass destruction. He built a dynasty. He's a 2x MVP, multiple-time champion, and universally respected, not for his size, but for his soul.

Steph Curry proved that heart and hard work beat hype every time.

Quotes from Steph Curry:

"Success is not an accident; success is actually a choice."

"Be the best version of yourself in anything that you do. You don't have to live anybody else's story."

"I can do all things."

"It's not about getting hot. It's about staying consistent."

"Basketball is not just a sport. It's a lifestyle. It's who I am."

"I try to make it look easy, but the behind-the-scenes work is where the magic happens."

"I prepare so no one can take what's mine."

"Every time I rise up, I have confidence that I'm going to make it."

"I've never been afraid of big moments. I get butterflies... I embrace them."

"I've always believed that if you put in the work, the results will come."

"Steph didn't just shoot his shot, he changed the game with it." — Ryan Stream

THE UNNAMED WARRIOR - The First Through the Door

In 2020, a quiet warrior made history. She became the first woman to graduate from the U.S. Army Special Forces Qualification Course—the same brutal, unforgiving "Q Course" that for decades had only seen men survive. She earned the Green Beret—not because she was a woman, but because she was a warrior.

There was no special treatment. No exceptions. No lowered standards. She completed the same course that breaks down some of the strongest men on earth. The Q Course is designed to expose every weakness—physical, mental, and spiritual. And still, she endured. She conquered. She passed.

Her name? Still classified. Because her goal wasn't fame. It was service. Her mission wasn't to prove a point, it was to complete one of the most elite training programs on earth and become a Special Forces operator.

But let's be clear—she wasn't the first woman to try. Back in 1980, Captain Kathleen Wilder became the first woman to complete the Army's Special Forces Officer Course. But due to internal politics and discrimination, she was denied graduation. She eventually received a certificate after filing a complaint—but was never allowed to serve in a Special Forces unit. Forty years later, history was rewritten.

The unnamed woman who earned her Green Beret in 2020 didn't just finish a course.

She shattered the idea that some dreams are off-limits based on gender. She didn't raise her voice—she raised the bar. This is Courage: When they say "You can't," You say "Watch me." When they say "No one like you ever has," You say "Then I'll go first."

When others need permission—you create the path.

Legendary Leadership Lesson: Lead even when no one looks like you.

"She earned everything. She's a soldier first—gender second." — U.S. Army Special Forces Official, 2020 (First Female Green Beret (Military / Courage Under Pressure)

Real courage isn't about proving people wrong—it's about proving your purpose right.

You don't need applause, approval, or permission to go first. You just need a mission and the guts to finish it.

The first woman to earn the Green Beret didn't need a spotlight. She needed grit.

She didn't show up to represent her gender—she showed up to represent excellence. She didn't talk about changing the game. She became the game-changer. If you want to lead like a legend, don't wait for the path.

Be the path.

TOM BRADY – The 199th Pick Who Became the Greatest Ever

Tom wasn't the strongest. He wasn't the fastest. He didn't have the rocket arm. At the NFL Combine, he ran a 5.28 forty-yard dash—slower than some offensive linemen. Teams passed on him over... and over... and over.

198 players were picked before him.

But Tom Brady didn't let that define him. He stored it, he carried it and he fueled himself with it. When he finally got drafted by the New England Patriots—sixth round, 199th overall, he walked into the front office and said:

"I'm the best decision this organization has ever made."

He believed it. Then he proved it.

When Drew Bledsoe went down with an injury, no one expected anything from the skinny backup. But Brady stepped in and never gave the job back.

7 Super Bowl rings later... the rest is history.

He wasn't built like a legend, but he became one.

And what made him great wasn't just wins—it was obsession. He studied harder, trained longer, slept better, ate cleaner, worked deeper. He turned doubt into a dynasty.

Tom Brady wasn't the GOAT because he was the most gifted—he was the most obsessed with greatness.

Lead Like a Legend: The 5 C's That Unlock Greatness

Quotes from Tom Brady:

"You want to know which ring is my favorite? The next one."

"I didn't come this far to only come this far."

"Every setback is just a setup for a comeback."

"You don't have to be the most talented. You just have to be the most relentless."

"I'm not a finished product. I'm still getting better."

"There's a lot of sacrifice. But if you want to be great, you can't have it both ways."

"You push your body to the limits, but it starts with your mind."

"Pressure is a privilege."

"You earn everything—every single day."

"I didn't get here because I dreamed it. I got here because I worked it."

"Brady didn't walk through the door a champion. He became one when no one was looking." — Ryan Stream

ALLEN IVERSON – The Answer Nobody Saw Coming

Allen was raised in poverty, surrounded by violence, and counted speak for himself. Allen Iverson wasn't supposed to make it out of Newport News, Virginia. He grew up in the projects, his mom, just a teenager trying to keep him alive, his world filled with more struggle than security.

Fuel for the Fight — Quotes to Lead, Rise, and Dominate

At seventeen, Iverson was facing fifteen years in prison after a bowling alley brawl. It nearly destroyed his life. But the truth is, he was set up, scapegoated, and sentenced without proper evidence. Public pressure eventually got him out, but not before the system tried to crush him.

When Georgetown gave him a shot, he didn't waste it. He balled like his life depended on it—because it did. Then he hit the NBA like lightning. Six feet tall. 165 pounds soaking wet. Surrounded by giants. And he cooked them all!

Iverson was more than a scorer; he was a cultural force. Cornrows. Tattoos. Swagger. Passion. He played hurt. He played angry. He played like every game was a fight to prove he belonged.

And when people criticized his style? His walk? His talk? He said: "I am who I am."

Allen Iverson didn't ask for permission, he showed up with purpose. And changed the league forever.

"I don't want to be Michael Jordan. I don't want to be Magic. I don't want to be Bird or Isiah. I don't want to be any of those guys. I want to look in the mirror and say I did it my way."

"I'd rather have more heart than talent."

"I play every game like it's my last."

"I've made a lot of mistakes, but I've never been a bad person."

"You can talk about practice, but I was out there dying in games."

Lead Like a Legend: The 5 C's That Unlock Greatness

"People don't understand the grind unless they've lived it."

"Everything I've been through made me who I am today."

"My game was never about just basketball. It was about surviving."

"They said I was too small. I showed them how big my heart was."

"The real ones know what I stood for."

"Iverson wasn't built like a champion. He bled like one. And the world couldn't look away." — Ryan Stream

COREY LEROY – The LeRoy Family Legacy

More than just viral stars, the LeRoys are a family of champions—on the field, on the court, and in life. Led by Cory LeRoy, a pilot and devoted father, their journey has inspired over 1.5 million subscribers with a message of faith, family, and fearless living. Their children are athletic standouts, driven by discipline and love—and they carry the strength of their brother Logan, who watches from heaven. The LeRoys prove that legacy isn't about fame—it's about rising, together.

"Doubt not. Fear not."— Cory LeRoy

RICARDO MARTINEZ

No one reading this can see my father-in-law the way I do.

I see him behind closed doors, late at night after a long day of hard work, or early in the morning before the sun rises. I see him when he's tired, when he's upset, when he's hurting moments when no one else is around.

He's a man who, even in his exhaustion, continues to serve. No matter what, he shows up with food or clothes, ready to give whatever he can to someone in need. If you're low on food around him, you won't stay hungry for long; your belly will be full. He is so funny, too, and you will have a great time around him! His personality is contagious.

His father passed away when he was young, and it was he who stepped up to pay for his family members' needs. He even paid for someone's college education until they graduated as a teacher—taking on responsibilities no one expected. His calloused hands tell the story of a life spent working relentlessly.

He was once a famous drummer, playing in front of thousands, on radio shows, and touring across the country. His talent, his heart, and his unwavering work ethic have shaped me into the musician I am today. He's helped me with tips, tricks, and has even been in all my country music videos as the drummer.

Today, he's a badass rancher, unbothered by the scorching heat or biting cold. He's always got a job to do, and no matter what, it gets done, correctly, without excuses.

His family came to America with absolutely nothing—just the clothes on their backs and the hope of achieving what we call the American Dream. And in that, they are heroes—true heroes.

Many people today are afraid to change their job, but my in-laws left everything they knew, crossed borders, and built a new life in a foreign land. In that sense, they were pioneers, just like those who came before us, braving the unknown for a chance at something better.

Because of their sacrifices, I was able to build my own life and family with their daughter. Without them, my family tree would not be as rich with life and love as it is today.

He has made my life better in ways words can't fully capture. I love this man, and I love his wife. They are two of the most incredible people I've ever known.

LORENA MARTINZ

A letter to my mother-in-law.

I've never met someone like you. You came into my life not just as a mother-in-law, but as someone who embraced me with arms wide open. You've loved me like a son—not out of obligation, but out of pure, genuine, unconditional love. And that kind of love? It's rare. It's powerful. And I've never taken it for granted.

You were once a young girl, afraid, I'm sure. Alone in many ways.

Crossing a border with nothing but hope in your heart, a dream in your soul, and—I'm sure—tears in your eyes. The world will never know the bravery you had to show or the fear you faced.

You didn't know what the future held, but you walked forward anyway. Running toward the giant!

Fuel for the Fight — Quotes to Lead, Rise, and Dominate

Is there a more legendary story than that? To leave everything behind…To become a citizen of a new country…To fight for a dream that didn't even exist yet.

That's courage. That's strength. That's the stuff heroes are made of.

And look what you built. You built a life. You built a homeland. You built a family that radiates light everywhere it goes.

You raised Carlos, a true cowboy—strong, bold, the kind of man we're all proud to know.

You raised Ricky, a man of peace, honor, and loyalty. A man who was flipped in a vehicle accident that nearly crushed him, yet he got back up. And every day since, he's worked tirelessly, not to impress anyone, but to make himself proud, and his wife McKenzie, who proudly serves in the military.

And then… you gave me your daughter. When I asked you and Ricardo for her hand, I wasn't just asking for permission,

I was stepping into a legacy. One that you helped shape with every late-night shift, every hotel room you cleaned, every hospital office you walked and scrubbed, every tear you cried, every prayer you whispered.

Now your daughter and I travel the world. We speak to crowds. Our music reaches across countries. We spread a message of kindness, hope, and unity. We break language barriers and cultural walls with nothing but a smile and a song.

But none of that would exist without you. Because of your sacrifice and the example, you set. Because you did the hard, the scary, and the impossible…

I have the life I have today. And to the reader, for a moment:

Can you imagine going to a country where you don't understand the language, and every day you cry because you're trying your best but feel invisible?

Can you imagine watching your kids go to school and struggle, and wanting so badly to help them with their homework, while you're just learning how to spell your own name in a new tongue?

Can you imagine working a job where people talk down to you, not because you lack intelligence or work ethic, but simply because you speak differently?

Life is hard enough. And yet… they showed up even when it was scary. Even when they were pointed at, laughed at, ignored. They showed up. That's what strength looks like. And it lives in people like Lorena Martinez.

Now look at you, working your way into the school system, making an impact every day in a new way. Still growing. Still serving. Still building. You and Ricardo have shown me something priceless: That you can come to a country without knowing the language and still make something of yourself.

That legends don't need a mansion, millions of dollars, or some flashy business card. Because what you do isn't about profit, it's about purpose and the legacy you leave in your children, the

Fuel for the Fight — Quotes to Lead, Rise, and Dominate

courage you pass on, and the love you pour into every generation that follows.

Because of you, my wife and I get to help millions. Because of you, our kids know what love, sacrifice, and strength really look like. We all play a part in our family tree. And your piece of the puzzle is sacred because of what you've carried, what you've endured, and what you've given—our family is a masterpiece.

We love you, Lorena Martinez.

Thank you for everything. You are, without question, one of the greatest legends!

Now, I get it, sometimes you don't have time to read a full chapter, but you still need that fire. You need fuel. For me? It's quotes. One good line can flip my mindset, shift my spirit, and get me back in the fight.

So here it is—quotes broken into fast-access sections for whatever kind of moment you're in:

When you need discipline

When you feel beat down

When you're trying to lead

When you need to remember God's got you

When you're ready to go beast mode

This chapter's your personal ammo box. Flip to it, find your fire, and get back in the game.

FUEL FOR THE FIGHT

"I have learned over the years that when one's mind is made up, this diminishes fear."— Rosa Parks

"Whether you think you can or you think you can't—you're right." — Henry Ford

"He who says he can, and he who says he can't be both usually right." — Confucius

"Do not pray for an easy life, pray for the strength to endure a difficult one." — Bruce Lee

"Success is not final; failure is not fatal: it is the courage to continue that counts." —Winston Churchill

"Every time I step on the floor, I want to make people remember me."— Caitlin Clark (Sports / NCAA Record Breaker)

"Strength does not come from physical capacity. It comes from an indomitable will." —Mahatma Gandhi

"The most important thing I've learned is that you're capable of way more than you think." — Katelyn Ohashi (Gymnast, viral floor routine phenom)

"Everything you've ever wanted is on the other side of fear." — George Addair

Fuel for the Fight — Quotes to Lead, Rise, and Dominate

"You become what you believe." — Oprah Winfrey

"Be disobedient to average.

You weren't born to fit in.

You were born to stand out—and shine" - Ben Kjar - World Champion Wrestler · Speaker · Entrepreneur

"I don't run away from a challenge because I am afraid. I run toward it because the only way to escape fear is to trample it beneath your feet." — Nadia Comăneci (Olympic Gymnast, first perfect 10)

"It's not about being the best. It's about being better than you were yesterday." — Jordyn Wieber (Olympic Gold Medallist)

"Fall seven times, stand up eight." — Japanese Proverb

"Pain is temporary. It may last a minute, or an hour, or a day… but if you quit, it lasts forever." — Lance Armstrong

"If I can do it, you can do it. First, you believe it's possible…Then, it becomes possible."— Nixeon Stream, 12-Year-Old, 7 states, 7 gold medals, 2x National s – ESPN Disney World Cheerleader Summit Champion

"Stand up for yourself" Olympia Stream 7 years Old. Motocross and Horseback riding.

"There is nothing noble in being superior to your fellow man; true nobility is being superior to your former self." — Ernest Hemingway

DISCIPLINE & DETERMINATION

"Discipline is the bridge between goals and accomplishment." — Jim Rohn

"You have to keep pushing. You have to keep dreaming. And you've got to believe you're enough—before the world ever tells you." — Morgan Hurd (World Champion Gymnast)

"We are what we repeatedly do. Excellence, then, is not an act, but a habit." — Aristotle

"Hard work beats talent when talent doesn't work hard." — Tim Notke

"It's okay to struggle. It's okay to fall apart. But never stop showing up for yourself."— Laurie Hernandez (Olympic Gymnast & Champion of Joy)

"Hard days are the best because that's when champions are made." — Gabby Douglas (Olympic All-Around Champion)

"If you're going through hell, keep going." — Winston Churchill

"The only limit to our realization of tomorrow is our doubts of today." — Franklin D. Roosevelt

Fuel for the Fight — Quotes to Lead, Rise, and Dominate

"You don't get stronger without resistance. You don't lead without falling. And you don't win without work." — Maggie Nichols (All-American Gymnast & Advocate)

"Every single practice matters. Every rep is building something. You don't win by chance—you win by choice." — Gabi Butler (World Champion Cheerleader, Netflix's "Cheer").

"If you want to be great, stop asking for permission." — Unknown

"You miss 100% of the shots you don't take." — Wayne Gretzky

"Success isn't always about greatness. It's about consistency." — Dwayne "The Rock" Johnson

"Don't sit down and wait for the opportunities to come. Get up and make them. — Madam C.J. Walker

"You don't find willpower, you create it." — Unknown

"Amateurs sit and wait for inspiration. The rest of us just get up and go to work." —Stephen King "I'd rather regret the risks that didn't work out than the chances I didn't take at all." — Simone Biles (Olympic Gymnast, GOAT)

FAITH, PURPOSE & INNER STRENGTH

"I can do all things through Christ who strengthens me." — Philippians 4:13

"Be still and know that I am God." — Psalm 46:10

"I am no bird; and no net ensnares me: I am a free human being with an independent will." — Charlotte Brontë

"Faith is taking the first step even when you don't see the whole staircase." — Martin Luther King Jr.

"With God, all things are possible." — Matthew 19:26

"When you go through deep waters, I will be with you." —Isaiah 43:2

"Don't worry about anything; instead, pray about everything." — Philippians 4:6

"Your talent is God's gift to you. What you do with it is your gift back to God." — Leo Buscaglia

"I came, I saw, God conquered." — Joan of Arc

"The will of God will never take you where the grace of God will not protect you." — Billy Graham

"Faith does not make things easy—it makes them possible." — Luke 1:37

"The Lord is my strength and my shield; my heart trusts in Him." — Psalm 28:7

LEADERSHIP & LEGACY

"Leadership is not about being in charge. It is about taking care of those in your charge." —Simon Sinek

"Power is not given to you. You have to take it."— Zenobia of Palmyra

"The function of leadership is to produce more leaders, not more followers." — Ralph Nader

Fuel for the Fight — Quotes to Lead, Rise, and Dominate

"Be kind. And always say hello first." — Olympia Stream, age 7

"Be real. Don't lie. Own it. You can't cover the sun with one finger. The truth always shines through." – Elizabeth Stream · Author · Business Owner · Model

"A genuine leader is not a searcher for consensus but a molder of consensus." — Martin Luther King Jr.

"They tried to bury us. They didn't know we were seeds." — Dolores Huerta

"To handle yourself, use your head; to handle others, use your heart." — Eleanor Roosevelt

"I do not like the word 'boss.' I much prefer the word 'leader.'"— Anna Bissell

"Better to die with Honor than to live in shame." — Queen Nzinga

"The greatest leader is not necessarily the one who does the greatest things. He is the one that gets people to do the greatest things." — Ronald Reagan

"You don't inspire your team by showing them how amazing you are. You inspire them by showing them how amazing they are." — Carly Patterson (Olympic Gold Medallist)

"Even if you kill me, I will die with my people. You will never break us." — Lozen, Apache Warrior

"A good leader takes a little more than his share of the blame, a little less than his share of the credit." — Arnold H. Glasow

"Leadership is practiced not so much in words as in attitude and in actions." — Harold S. Geneen

"You may have the weapons, but I have the will of my ancestors." — Yaa Asantewaa

"A queen is not afraid to die for her kingdom." — Queen Tomyris

"Live as if you were to die tomorrow. Learn as if you were to live forever." — Mahatma Gandhi

"Legacy is not leaving something for people. It's leaving something in people." — Peter Strople

"The best way to find yourself is to lose yourself in the service of others." — Mahatma Gandhi

ERIC THOMAS (ET THE HIP HOP PREACHER)

"When you want to succeed as bad as you want to breathe, then you'll be successful."

"Don't make a habit out of choosing what feels good over what's actually good for you."

"Everybody wants to be a beast, until it's time to do what beasts do."

"Some of you love sleep more than you love success."

"You're not failing. You're forming."

"Pain is temporary. Quitting lasts forever."

"I can. I will. I must."

Fuel for the Fight — Quotes to Lead, Rise, and Dominate

"Be phenomenal or be forgotten."

"You will not outwork me."

"Average skill with phenomenal will."

BONUS FROM RYAN STREAM

"Your story is part of His strategy."

"Lead like a legend."

"You don't need permission to lead. Just purpose."

"Comfort kills dreams—and it buries legacies."

"They threw stones—I built the throne."

"Fail until failure becomes your fuel."

"Your standards are a direct reflection of your life.

Look at your body. Your habits. Your relationships. Your bank account.

You don't rise to the level of your goals—you fall to the level of your standards.

Raise them, and your entire life rises with them."

"Don't assume- ask with love. Because guessing leads to resentment. Talking leads to Understanding."

NOW, GO AND LEAD LIKE A LEGEND!

"Leadership is practiced not so much in words as in attitude and in actions." — Harold S. Geneen

"You may have the weapons, but I have the will of my ancestors." — Yaa Asantewaa

"A queen is not afraid to die for her kingdom." — Queen Tomyris

"Live as if you were to die tomorrow. Learn as if you were to live forever." — Mahatma Gandhi

"Legacy is not leaving something for people. It's leaving something in people." — Peter Strople

"The best way to find yourself is to lose yourself in the service of others." — Mahatma Gandhi

ERIC THOMAS (ET THE HIP HOP PREACHER)

"When you want to succeed as bad as you want to breathe, then you'll be successful."

"Don't make a habit out of choosing what feels good over what's actually good for you."

"Everybody wants to be a beast, until it's time to do what beasts do."

"Some of you love sleep more than you love success."

"You're not failing. You're forming."

"Pain is temporary. Quitting lasts forever."

"I can. I will. I must."

Fuel for the Fight — Quotes to Lead, Rise, and Dominate

"Be phenomenal or be forgotten."

"You will not outwork me."

"Average skill with phenomenal will."

BONUS FROM RYAN STREAM

"Your story is part of His strategy."

"Lead like a legend."

"You don't need permission to lead. Just purpose."

"Comfort kills dreams—and it buries legacies."

"They threw stones—I built the throne."

"Fail until failure becomes your fuel."

"Your standards are a direct reflection of your life.

Look at your body. Your habits. Your relationships. Your bank account.

You don't rise to the level of your goals—you fall to the level of your standards.

Raise them, and your entire life rises with them."

"Don't assume- ask with love. Because guessing leads to resentment. Talking leads to Understanding."

NOW, GO AND LEAD LIKE A LEGEND!